THE WITCH
OF EDMONTON

William Rowley,
Thomas Dekker & John Ford

MANCHESTER
1824

Manchester University Press

REVELS STUDENT EDITIONS

Based on the highly respected Revels Plays, which provide a wide range of scholarly critical editions of plays by Shakespeare's contemporaries, the Revels Student Editions offer readable and competitively priced introductions, text and commentary designed to distil the erudition and insights of the Revels Plays, while focusing on matters of clarity and interpretation. These editions are aimed at undergraduates, graduate teachers of Renaissance drama and all those who enjoy the vitality and humour of one of the world's greatest periods of drama.

GENERAL EDITOR David Bevington

Dekker/Rowley/Ford *The Witch of Edmonton*
Fletcher *The Tamer Tamed; or, The Woman's Prize*
Ford *'Tis Pity She's a Whore*
Jonson *Bartholomew Fair*
Jonson *Volpone*
Jonson *Masques of Difference: Four Court Masques*
Kyd *The Spanish Tragedy*
Marlowe *The Jew of Malta*
Marlowe *Tamburlaine the Great*
Marston *The Malcontent*
Middleton *Women Beware Women*
Middleton/Rowley *The Changeling*
Middleton/Tourneur *The Revenger's Tragedy*
Webster *The Duchess of Malfi*
Webster *The White Devil*

Plays on Women: An Anthology
Middleton *A Chaste Maid in Cheapside*
Middleton/Dekker *The Roaring Girl*
Anon. *Arden of Faversham*
Heywood *A Woman Killed with Kindness*

REVELS STUDENT EDITIONS

THE WITCH
OF EDMONTON

William Rowley,
Thomas Dekker & John Ford

Edited by Peter Corbin & Douglas Sedge

based on The Revels Plays Companion Library edition of
Three Jacobean Witchcraft Plays
edited by Peter Corbin & Douglas Sedge
published by Manchester University Press, 1986

MANCHESTER
UNIVERSITY PRESS

Introduction, critical apparatus, etc.
© Peter Corbin & Douglas Sedge 1997

The right of Peter Corbin & Douglas Sedge to be identified as the editors
of this work has been asserted by them in accordance with the Copyright,
Designs and Patents Act 1988.

Published by Manchester University Press
Altrincham Street, Manchester M1 7JA

www.manchesteruniversitypress.co.uk

British Library Cataloguing-in-Publication Data
A catalogue record for this book is available from the British Library

ISBN 978 0 7190 5247 7 *paperback*

First published 1999

008

Printed in Great Britain by
TJ Books Limites, Padstow

Contents

Acknowledgements

This edition is a thoroughly revised version of the text which appeared in our anthology *Three Jacobean Witchcraft Plays* (Revels Plays Companion Library, 1986). We have taken the opportunity to reconsider some textual readings, to revise the punctuation and extend and modify stage directions. We have also amplified the commentary notes and included in an appendix the whole of Goodcole's pamphlet *The Wonderful Discovery of Elizabeth Sawyer* of 1621. The introduction has been extensively re-written to take into account the recent critical debate about the play and its treatment of witchcraft. A section on Further Reading is provided.

We are indebted to the General Editor, David Bevington, for his vigilance, sagacity and encouragement.

Introduction

Modern historians have variously interpreted early modern witch-craft belief in terms of the customs of vestigial paganism transmitted via folklore, simple superstition or a deep-rooted desire to retain the half-understood practices and rituals of Roman Catholicism in the face of the Protestant Reformation. Recent developments in critical theory have made witchcraft an area of sharp controversy. Some critics with a feminist perspective have seen the persecution of witches in early modern Europe in terms of 'gendercide', a vast programme of mass murder organised by an oppressive male hierar-chy, a sort of Holocaust in which it has been claimed that nine million died. Recent scholarship suggests that the reality, while undeniably horrendous, was less clear-cut and more complex. For example, over the whole of Europe there were perhaps one hundred thousand witch trials between 1450 and 1750, resulting in forty to fifty thousand executions, of which twenty to twenty-five per cent were of men. In England, ninety per cent of those accused of witchcraft were women, but the number of executions was far lower than on the continent.[1] Although it is difficult to draw any secure conclusions because of the incomplete nature of archive material, it has recently been suggested that the total number of those executed might have been less than five hundred.[2]

Although a subject of fierce academic debate in the late twentieth century, for Jacobean society witchcraft presented a real and fright-ening danger which posed a threat to everyone from the highest to the lowest in the land. A pamphlet of 1591, *News from Scotland, Declaring the Damnable Life and Death of Doctor Fian*,[3] relates how witchcraft placed King James in mortal danger on his voyage from Denmark with his new Queen in 1590. The children of the scholar and gentleman Edward Fairfax, the translator of Tasso, were alleged to have been bewitched in 1621 by six women who lived in Knaresborough Forest;[4] and at numerous trials countless ordinary people testified to their belief that they had suffered from witchcraft practices. Many of those who attended the first performances of

1

plays dealing with witchcraft, such as Shakespeare's *Macbeth* (1606), Middleton's *The Witch* (*c.*1609–16) and Brome's *The Late Lancashire Witches* (1634), would have accepted the notion of the devil's direct intervention in the affairs of men and women and the attempt by individuals to invoke his personal assistance. An incident relating to the performance of Marlowe's *Dr Faustus* at Exeter illustrates this point memorably, for in the course of the presentation certain of the actors were incapacitated by the conviction that 'there was one devil too many amongst them; and so after a little pause desired the people to pardon them, they could go no further with this matter; the people also understanding the thing as it was, every man hastened to be first out of doors'.[5]

English judicial attitudes and practice towards witchcraft were comparatively tolerant compared to those common on the continent and in Scotland. It was not until 1563 that the first comprehensive act was passed specifically directed towards witchcraft and, significantly, although bewitching to death attracted the death penalty, injuring persons or goods or cattle and seeking treasure warranted only prison and pillory for the first offences; the second conviction, however, rendered the criminal liable to execution. That political considerations were of major importance is evidenced by a subsequent clarification to the act which nominates astrological calculation and divination of the length of the Queen's life as indictable offences. The law was strengthened under James I. The act of 1604 makes the keeping of familiars an offence, together with the exhumation of bodies for conjuration or evocation. In contrast to continental practice English witches were almost always examined by Justices rather than by officials of the church, and the accused were usually examined on factual evidence rather than hearsay. Horrendous tortures, practised on the continent, to elicit confession and to determine guilt, which have coloured modern perceptions of such trials (as in Caryl Churchill's play *Vinegar Tom*), were not common experience in England. The penalty, should a trial lead to conviction of a capital offence, was death by hanging, not by burning.

Whilst we may accept that English justice was less savage than that of neighbouring countries, it must be admitted that a society, often facing unforeseen and unaccountable natural disasters, such as crop failures, cattle sickness, etc., was inclined to seek out its scapegoats amongst the weakest and most vulnerable. Women, especially the elderly and deprived, often became the objects of gossip and fear, and thus the subjects of persecution. Not infrequently suspicion of witchcraft had its roots in longstanding social friction between families or individuals, and in very many cases trials were instigated by the testimony of other women.[6]

A work which influenced views on witchcraft and demonology in the seventeenth century and subsequently is *Malleus Maleficarum* (*'The Hammer of Witches'*). Published in 1486, this misogynistic work was designed by its authors, Jacob Sprenger and Heinrich Kramer (Institor), to provide a *summa* of witchcraft and its practices, and a set of procedures for the discovery, examination, torture and trial of witches. To what extent the work was a response to or a provocation of the witch hysteria which swept the continent, and especially Germany, in the late fifteenth and sixteenth centuries is open to argument; but by means of its many reprintings it initiated a lengthy, complex and sharp debate between the absolute believers in witchcraft and those who were more sceptically inclined.

Although England largely escaped witch-mania until the later sixteenth century, the controversy was eventually taken up by many English writers. Reginald Scot, sceptical of the claims made against witches, published *The Discovery of Witchcraft* (1584) soon after the witch trials at St Osyth in 1582, and argued against the unwarranted persecution of the old and simple-minded who were frequently branded as witches. Subsequently, the nonconforming preacher George Gifford published his *A Discourse of the Subtle Practices of Devils* in 1587 and *A Dialogue concerning Witches and Witchcrafts* in 1593, works which also demonstrate considerable scepticism. He argues that the devil has no need for old women to do his work and that much innocent blood may be shed because of unreliable confessions. Such views were vigorously opposed. King James VI of Scotland's *Demonology* (1597) was expressly written against Scot, whose *Discovery* was banned immediately on James's accession to the English throne in 1603. King James's absolutist stance, although qualified in later years, owed much to continental theory, and was supported, if not surpassed in its vehemence, by the Puritan William Perkins, whose *Discourse of the Damned Art of Witchcraft* was published in 1608.

The dramatists' source for the Elizabeth Sawyer story was a pamphlet written by Henry Goodcole, *The Wonderful Discovery of Elizabeth Sawyer a Witch, late of Edmonton* (1621), which followed hard upon the events themselves.[7] Goodcole, the chaplain who heard Sawyer's confession in Newgate Gaol, appears to have made a practice of publishing pamphlets which relate criminal confessions. (In 1618 he had published a pamphlet which contained details of the conversion of one Francis Robinson, who had attempted to counterfeit the great seal of England and was subsequently hanged, drawn and quartered.) His later pamphlet offers a painstaking interrogation of Elizabeth Sawyer in which she acknowledges her relationship with the devil in the form of a dog and repents her sins. The pamphlet takes a moral stance and is designed to present the reader with exemplary counsel, so that it is difficult to assess its documentary status. The dramatists draw quite closely on some of the details of Gooodcole's report but significantly depart from his account in shaping the material for their own dramatic purposes. For example, whilst in the pamphlet Sawyer is married with a family, the play presents her as entirely isolated without communal support, and whereas she asserts in the pamphlet that the dog appeared to her sometimes as black and sometimes as white, the dramatists use the variation to signify the Dog's betrayal. The dramatists' freedom with the source material establishes Sawyer's social vulnerability and thus generates a more personal level of sympathy for her than is available to readers of Goodcole's 1621 pamphlet. It also enables them to introduce a measure of scepticism found in the wide contemporary debate on the subject of witchcraft itself.

The play, which has been described as 'a comprehensive study of Elizabethan ideas of witchcraft'[8] and 'the soberest and most factual of all witch plays',[9] dramatises an extensive range of commonly accepted witchcraft practice. Elizabeth Sawyer's physical appearance and social status provide a stereotypical image; 'poor, deformed and ignorant / And like a bow buckled and bent together' (2.1.3–4), she has only one eye (2.1.96–7), is old and is isolated from the community. This directly conforms with Scot's observation in *The Discovery of Witchcraft* in which he notes that those who are said to be witches 'are women who are commonly old, lame, blear-eyed, foul and full of wrinkles; poor, sullen, superstitious . . . They are doting, scolds, mad, devilish' (1.3). Sawyer certainly has a scolding tongue which she uses with effect in her confrontations with Old Banks (2.1) and with Sir Arthur Clarington and the Justice (4.1), and finally on her way to the scaffold in the play's final movement. Her poverty and related social isolation initially generate conflict with Old Banks over her right to collect firewood, but it soon becomes apparent that he is not alone in stigmatising her; Young Banks, his morris companions and many others also see her as a witch. Driven out of the community, she accepts the role when it is offered by the devil-dog (2.1.128 ff.) and, under some compulsion, adopts traditional witchcraft behaviour. The devil-dog, Tommy, becomes her familiar and companion for whom she shows considerable affection, and reference is made in the text to his habit of sucking her blood from a witch's teat or mark, in a perverse travesty of motherhood. He then threatens her, and subsequently abandons her when she is finally condemned. In her career as a witch, Sawyer exhibits characteristic behaviour in her desire to employ Dog to assist her in punishing those who have slighted her: Old Banks, Anne Ratcliffe, etc. Dog is ordered to 'touch' her enemies. Although Old Banks and his son are beyond Dog's influence, Anne Ratcliffe is not, for she is driven mad and subsequently dies:

> [*Dog touches Anne Ratcliffe.*]
> *Anne Ratcliffe.* Oh, my ribs are made of a paned hose, and they break.
> There's a Lancashire hornpipe in my throat. Hark how it tickles it, with
> doodle, doodle, doodle, doodle!   (4.1.204–7)

Witches were believed to be able to 'touch' victims, and thus destroy them, or deliver *maleficia* in a variety of ways, if they could get close to their targets, so condemning them to death, disease or madness. There were counter-measures. It was considered possible to summon forcibly, and thus discover, a witch by firing the thatch of the suspect's house (4.1.19–31), whilst 'touching' might be reversed if the victim could in some way draw the witch's blood by 'scratching' her or his body (4.1.198).[10] Thus *The Witch of Edmonton* dramatises both common belief in witchcraft and also the scepticism of Scot and others, such reservations being articulated particularly in 4.1.

THEATRICAL CONTEXT

The title-page of the first and only early edition of *The Witch of Edmonton*, published in 1658, gives the authors as '*William Rowley, Thomas Dekker, John Ford, &c.*'. Many Renaissance plays found their way into print for the first time during the interregnum period (1642–60) when stage performances were forbidden by the Puritan authorities and reading a text became the chief, if not only, way to experience these works. The play dates, however, from 1621, for there is a record of a performance at court on 29 December of that year. The play includes a dramatisation of the events which led to the execution of Elizabeth Sawyer on 19 April in the same year. No doubt the play received its first performance at the Cockpit Theatre as soon as possible after that sensation, since Prince Charles's Company would have wished to capitalise on the scandal while it was still fresh in people's minds. Such opportunism was quite common during this period. For example, the three named co-authors of this play were involved (together with John Webster) only three years later in another notoriously topical play entitled *The Late Murder of the Son upon the Mother, or Keep the Widow Waking*, a play which is now lost to us but of which we know some of the scandalous details from the court case which reported the events.

Since swiftness of completion was an especially important factor in such plays, it is not surprising that as many as three collaborators might be involved in the production of the script. Indeed, in view of the title-page's '&c.' after the three named authors, it is quite possible that there were other contributors to the text. Much scholarly ink has been expended on the dramatists' individual responsibilities for particular parts of the text, but it is generally agreed that Dekker was the overall leader of the project, having the main responsibility for the Elizabeth Sawyer area of the play, whilst Ford's hand is most apparent in the Frank Thorney plot and Rowley's main contribution lies in the Cuddy Banks scenes. It should be borne in mind, though, that the nature of collaborative work makes it difficult to resolve precisely questions of attribution, and such issues are largely irrelevant to the dramatic quality of a text. Many of the finest plays of the period were written in collaboration, and it is misleading to assume that such origins lead to poorly constructed plays.[11]

INTERPRETATIONS

The Play as domestic tragedy

Whilst it is important to situate *The Witch of Edmonton* within the context of Renaissance witchcraft and its specific practices, the play may also be explored as an example of domestic tragedy, a subgenre especially popular around the turn of century. Such plays as *Arden of Faversham* (1592), *A Warning for Fair Women* (1599), *A Woman Killed with Kindness* (1603), *The Miseries of Enforced Marriage* (1606) and *The Yorkshire Tragedy* (1608) portray the passions and crimes of ordinary folk in their everyday world, contrasting with the fall of kings and nations, the subject of most tragedies of the period. It was characteristic of domestic tragedy that a sensational crime, usually a murder associated with the breaking of marriage bonds, provided the play's central incident. Such source material was often drawn from popular pamphlets which related in colourful and gruesome detail a recent horrifying crime, together with confessions from the condemned cell or speeches from the scaffold. Based on such newsworthy events, these plays, the equivalent of modern docu-drama, were designed to capitalise on the fierce interest which such incidents aroused. Like modern tabloids, however, whilst the plays emphasised the wickedness of the crimes they depicted they also titillated and thrilled their audiences with astounding, vicarious experience of crime and passion in recognisable and familiar settings. In a society without regular newspapers or other media the players could present the intrigue, murder and discovery in so lively a form that, as Heywood reports in *An Apology for Actors*, fresh crimes might be discovered:

We will prove it by a domestic and home-born truth which within these few years happened. At Lin, in Norfolk, the then Earl of Sussex' players acting the old History of Feyer Francis, and presenting a woman who, insatiately doting on a young gentleman (the more securely to enjoy his affection) mischievously and secretly murdered her husband, whose ghost haunted her; and, at divers times, in her most solitary and private contemplations, in most horrid and fanciful shapes, appeared and stood before her. As this was acted, a towns-woman (till then of good estimation and report) finding her conscience (at this presentment) extremely troubled, suddenly screeched and cried out, 'Oh! my husband! I see the ghost of my husband fiercely threatening and menacing me!'

In this way the crime and murderer were revealed. Although Heywood is seeking to present the actors as moral agents—he has his own agenda in defending them against Puritan criticism—nevertheless the anecdote suggests the didactic power of the theatre. Certainly many domestic tragedies possess a strongly religious and moralistic tone due in part to their dramatic structure based in a pattern of sin, discovery and repentance.

Although *The Witch of Edmonton* (1621) was written a decade or more after the flowering of domestic drama, it generally reflects the conventions of the genre. The dramatists find their source for the Elizabeth Sawyer episodes in Goodcole's pamphlet, allegedly derived from conversations in Newgate Prison, and the play is precisely located in a specific environment. The rural setting of Jacobean Edmonton and its surroundings, supported by references to neighbouring villages such as Enfield and Waltham and to districts and locations in nearby London, ensures the audience's familiarity with the play-world. The dramatists create a sharply detailed evocation of the life of the community, its social structure, concerns and activities. A local knight, Sir Arthur Clarington, stands at the pinnacle of the social hierarchy, whilst beneath him are ranged minor gentry, yeomen, tenant farmers, and country men and women. Elizabeth Sawyer lives on the margins of this society; isolated, destitute and dependent, she is both feared and abused by her neighbours. It is a coherent but self-absorbed community in which social divisions and financial standing are clearly demarcated. The Thorneys, minor gentry, are bankrupt and obliged to repair their fortune by dowry-hunting. Thus Frank Thorney is drawn into crime by contracting a bigamous marriage with the daughter of a wealthy yeoman farmer, Old Carter. Though socially inferior to the Thorneys, Old Carter is proud of his yeoman status and his hard-won prosperity:

> No gentleman I, Master Thorney; spare the Mastership, call me by my name, John Carter. Master is a title my father, nor his before him, were acquainted with. Honest Hertfordshire yeomen, such an one am I.
>
> (1.2.3–6)

In sharp contrast to Thorney's indigence, Old Carter is able to deliver his daughter's dowry not in bonds or promissory notes but with immediate payment. A strong sense of his practical intelligence, common sense and direct engagement with the world of affairs is created via his language and particularly through his constant recourse to proverbial wisdom. However, farmers such as Old Banks and his neighbours are less successful and secure. Concern at a horse's sickness or fears for the health of the cattle (4.1.1–18) reveal a society living on the margin between prosperity and disaster and thus vulnerable and open to the conclusion that witchcraft is the cause of each misfortune—a set of conditions which drives them to witch-mania.

Bigamy, murder and witchcraft are the transgressions which threaten to dissever the social bonds of the play-world. The relationships between parents and children, servants and masters, husbands and wives are all threatened by the devil in the form of the Dog. Yet the sense of common loss in murder and execution together with the shared social rituals, exemplified by the morris dance and marriage celebration, provide a counter-sense of communal texture and solidarity which support the play's final movement in which the whole community is drawn together in grief. In this manner the play moves through a didactically organised patterning from Frank's bigamous deception and murder, to the discovery of the crime and his trial and execution which is presented as a cause of general lamentation, even including Old Carter:

> *Old Carter.* Go thy ways. I did not think to have shed one tear for thee, but thou hast made me water my plants spite of my heart.—Master Thorney, cheer up, man. Whilst I can stand by you, you shall not want help to keep you from falling. We have lost our children, both on's the wrong way, but we cannot help it. Better or worse, 'tis now as 'tis.
> *Old Thorney.* I thank you, sir. You are more kind than I
> Have cause to hope or look for. (5.3.143–51)

Although the text presents her as a victim of the devil's machinations, Elizabeth Sawyer's execution is presented without sentimentality. Her final speeches display anger and bitterness both with her accusers and with the devil who has deceived her:

> *Old Carter.* Thou'dst best confess all truly.
> *Elizabeth Sawyer.* Yet again?
> Have I scarce breath enough to say my prayers,
> And would you force me to spend that in bawlng?
> Bear witness. I repent all former evil;
> There is no damnèd conjuror like the devil. (5.3.48–52)

Her passage to execution, however, entirely complements Frank Thorney's. Both characters present, at a simple level, different but related exempla. Sawyer's story illustrates how anger, resentment and an unbridled tongue can allow the devil to gain entry to the world. Young Thorney's suggests that weakness of spirit, a wish to take the line of least resistance, can have equally disastrous consequences, and consequences which, unlike Sawyer, affect families, friends and others across the community.

At one level the play can be interpreted as a moralistic lesson which offers a straightforward, simple analysis of the way evil enters the world. But since it is a play which dramatises a range of viewpoints and dilemmas, rather than a sermon which argues from a single position, it offers a more complex dramatic experience. The play in performance, depending on the directorial line, can provoke intense sympathy for Elizabeth Sawyer, as a victim, over and against audience indignation at Young Thorney's compassionless duplicity.

The presentation of the witch

The witch theme is introduced into *The Witch of Edmonton* only at the beginning of the second act, the first act being taken up with Frank Thorney's secret marriage to Winnifride and his slide into bigamy with his betrothal, encouraged both by his father and by Old Carter, to Carter's daughter Susan. Sawyer's arrival in the play is in striking contrast to the way in which Frank has been presented. Frank has been hedged with social relationships from the very out-set—his new bride, his master, his father, his prospective father-in-law, second bride, her sister and even other suitors to Carter's daughters—and when he leaves the stage at the end of Act 1, albeit full of foreboding, it is to a meal with Carter, his family and associates.

Elizabeth Sawyer's social position and appearance precisely con-form to the common image of the witch. She is old, isolated from the community (the dramatists make no mention of her having a hus-band and children as in their source material), physically deformed ('like a bow buckled and bent together' (2.1.4), and she has only one eye (2.1.96–7). Thus she is a classic case for victimisation as a witch. As late as 1646 John Gaule, in *Select Cases of Conscience touching Witches and Witchcrafts*, recognised the fact that

> every old woman with a wrinkled face, a furred brow, a hairy lip, a gobber tooth, a squint eye, a squeaking voice, or a scolding tongue, having a ragged coat on her back, a skull-cap on her head, a spindle in her hand, and a dog or cat by her side; is not only suspected, but pronounced for a witch.[12]

The basic subsistence level of Sawyer's existence is emphasised by her activity of gathering sticks. She is given direct access to the audience, here and elsewhere, by her complaints which are sharp-tongued and contain a mixture of self-justification and audience challenge:

> And why on me? Why should the envious world
> Throw all their scandalous malice upon me?
> 'Cause I am poor, deformed and ignorant,
> And like a bow buckled and bent together.   (2.1.1–4)

Her speech provides an explanation of the social causes which have led to her ostracism and demonisation,[13] and also a sharp refusal to allow society to purify itself by scapegoating her:

> Must I for that be made a common sink
> For all the filth and rubbish of men's tongues
> To fall and run into?   (2.1.6–8)

Not for the last time in the play she speaks with a satirical edge and articulacy which goes beyond what one might regard as fitting to her naturalistic status. Indeed she gives us an acute demonstration of the processes by which she is being turned into a witch. Persecution and ill-treatment directly motivate her *malificia* as she seeks revenge for injuries and insults in a way which accords closely with common expectations of witch behaviour.[14] Her claims that society has created her 'bad tongue' and enforced a role upon her are confirmed by the immediate entry of Old Banks, who addresses her as 'witch' and 'hag' (as do the Morris Dancers later in this scene), deprives her of common charity by making her throw down her sticks, and, when she curses him, repays her with repeated beating.

Her malevolence towards Banks is thus in part justified by the treatment which he metes out to her. Thus she falls into witchcraft though ignorant of witchcraft practices:

> Call me hag and witch!
> What is the name? Where and by what art learned?
> What spells, what charms or invocations
> May the thing called Familiar be purchased?   (2.1.33–6)

She expresses her desire to become a witch in order to revenge herself on Old Banks:

> I have heard old beldams
> Talk of familiars in the shape of mice,
> Rats, ferrets, weasels and I wot not what,
> That have appeared and sucked, some say, their blood.   (2.1.109–12)

Her wild and random casting about for the means to become a witch—

> Would some power, good or bad,
> Instruct me which way I might be revenged
> Upon this churl, I'd go out of myself . . .
> Abjure all goodness, be at hate with prayer,
> And study curses, imprecations,
> Blasphemous speeches, oaths, detested oaths,
> Or anything that's ill   (2.1.114–22)

—contrasts markedly with the precise and learned conjuring of Dr Faustus in Marlowe's play or, on a lighter note, the diligent Fitzdottrel's attempts at devil-raising in Jonson's *The Devil is an Ass.*

The devil's entry in the shape of a black dog at this point ('Ho! Have I found thee cursing? Now thou art mine own', 2.1.128) closely follows Goodcole's pamphlet account in *The Wonderful Discovery of*

Elizabeth Sawyer on which this part of the plot is based. Despite the Dog's immediate offer of service, Sawyer gets very short shrift when she demands, as his first act of service, Old Banks's death. The Dog claims that his powers are circumscribed, for he can act only against the clearly wicked and Sawyer has to be content with more common *malificia* 'on his corn and cattle'. Thus the discrepancy between her expectations and what the devil is willing to deliver is an index of her exploitation, confirming her malleability and stressing her status as victim.

Certainly, her grasp of *malificia* is presented as being highly insecure. This is suggested by the various ways in which she articulates the Latin phrase which the Dog teaches her. Each time she attempts to utter the phrase '*Sanctibicetur nomem tuum*' her pronunciation changes,[15] even reversing the sense whilst claiming her expertise: '*Contaminetur nomen tuum*. I'm an expect scholar, / Speak Latin, or I know not well what language' (2.1.189–90). Goodcole's pamphlet confirms such ignorance, where she is reported as saying that she was not taught the Latin words by anyone but 'by the Devil alone; neither do I understand the meaning of these words nor can speak any more Latin words'.[16]

Should then Sawyer be seen primarily as a victim of the devil? Or is she to be held responsible for the tragic events which occur in Edmonton? Answers to such questions are necessarily interpretative, and it is a measure of the dramatic balance which the play achieves that it is possible to incline to an affirmative answer to both questions. The manner in which the men in 4.1 call Sawyer to account for the disasters which have overtaken the community would seem to suggest that she is a scapegoat. Their behaviour resembles the mentality of the lynch-mob as she is cited as the cause of the current spate of disasters which have disrupted the community: the blighted harvest and the sexual rebellion of the women, 'Our cattle fall, our wives fall, our daughters fall and maidservants fall' (4.1.15–16). Their resort to an entrenched superstition—that witches will come if the thatch of their cottage is fired—might seem to further this impression, but the dramatic presentation is intriguingly even-handed since, whether by accident or direct cause, their action is effective in producing her presence. The resulting mass outcry against Sawyer, '*All*. Out, witch! Beat her, kick her, set fire on her!' (4.1.33), is, however, tempered by the entry of the Justice whose scepticism deflates the witch-hunting mood:

Come, come. Firing her thatch? Ridiculous! Take heed, sirs, what you do.
Unless your proofs come better armed, instead of turning her into a witch,
you'll prove yourselves stark fools.   (4.1.48–51)

The Justice, since he is never given a personal name in the text, is
lent a measure of impartiality. It seems to be a considered irony that
he remains staunchly sceptical of the accusations against Sawyer
until she unwittingly brings suspicion upon herself by a generalised
satirical account of the corruption of 'men-witches' in society. One
detail from this scatter-gun attack touches, presumably accidentally,
on Sir Arthur Clarington's own vice (his seduction of Winnifride).
This persuades him that Sawyer has acquired the supernatural
powers of intuition attributed to witches, leading him to assure
the Justice of her guilt.

The presentation of her continuing relationship with her familiar,
the devil-dog, stresses both her vulnerability and spitefulness in
almost equal measure. Michael Hattaway has observed that it would
not have been permissible to present on a contemporary stage the
action of the Dog sucking Sawyer's teat,[17] but regardless of whether
Elizabeth Sawyer's denial of this 'reward' to the Dog is a result of the
dramatists' fear of the Jacobean censor, there is an intimacy in her
relationship with her devilish companion which may be even more
disturbing:

Stand on thy hind-legs up. Kiss me, my Tommy,
And rub away some wrinkles on my brow
By making my old ribs to shrug for joy
Of thy fine tricks. . . . Let's tickle.   (4.1.170–3)

Sawyer treats the Dog as if he were a human lover rather than a
dog—a more homely and less exotic equivalent of Faustus's offstage
copulation with the demon who impersonates Helen of Troy in
Marlowe's play *Dr Faustus*. In a later scene, there is no mistaking the
erotic nature of the language which Sawyer soliloquises when la-
menting her lover-dog's undue absence:[18]

                         Oh, my best love!
I am on fire, even in the midst of ice,
Raking my blood up till my shrunk knees feel
Thy curled head leaning on them. Come then, my darling!
If in the air thou hover'st, fall upon me
In some dark cloud.   (5.1.9–14)

Once again her language soars beyond her normal register to poeticise her affections, including an allusion to one of Zeus's most notable seductions, and her prizing of her lover above all earthly things stresses both her recklessness and her vulnerability:

> So that my bulch
> Show but his swarth cheek to me, let earth cleave
> And break from hell, I care not!   (5.1.18–20)

This lack of restraint is evident in the *maleficium* she pursues against one of her neighbours, which is far more serious than the comparatively trivial revenges which Tom has hitherto effected in her name. Sawyer, in urging the Dog to 'touch' Ann Ratcliffe, who has already been driven mad in revenge for a trivial dispute, achieves a shocking outcome, reported by Ratcliffe's husband:

> How now! What's become of her?
> *Old Ratcliffe.* Nothing. She's become nothing but the miserable trunk of a wretched woman. We were in her hands as reeds in a mighty tempest. Spite of our strengths away she brake, and nothing in her mouth being heard but 'the devil, the witch, the witch, the devil', she beat out her own brains, and so died.   (4.1.220–6)

However, the horror of this account seems to suggest an outcome which goes well beyond anything attributable to Sawyer's spitefulness; and although she looks forward to further deaths—she urges the Dog to fly at Sir Arthur and 'pluck out his throat'—the manner in which she exits with the Dog places the emphasis on further intimacies:

> Come, let's home and play.
> Our black work ended, we'll make holiday.   (4.1.294–5)

Such anticipations hardly suggest that she comprehends the nature of the 'black work' which is being performed. The impression given to the reader or audience may well be that she has in fact become the tool of the devil-dog. As the Spirit conjured up by the Dog in the shape of Susan comments: 'Th' witch pays for all' (3.1.88).

The devil-dog as internal dramatist

The impression of the devil-dog as controller of the action is strengthened by the presentation of Frank's murder of Susan, in what may be considered the main plot of the play. Startling as it is, the death of Anne Ratcliffe is something of a side issue, but that of Susan is unquestioningly central. This event is not part of Elizabeth Sawyer's campaign of spite against her neighbours, and thus raises the question of human responsibility over and against demonic control in its most acute form in the play. Who kills Susan? Is the devil-dog the real murderer?

The gravity of Frank's situation, when he has contracted himself bigamously to both Winnifride and Susan, is brought out in his words which echo Sawyer's compact with the devil:

When I was sold, I sold myself again —
Some knaves have done't in lands, and I in body.   (3.2.27–8)

It is important to note that although morally compromised he seems not to have any premeditated intent of harming Susan physically. Much depends on how we interpret the Dog's cryptic announcement at the beginning of 3.3: 'The mind's about it now'. If taken to apply to Frank, this statement might seem to suggest that the Dog is merely reflecting what is going on in Frank's subconscious mind. However, his further comment to the audience, 'One touch from me / Soon sets the body forward' (3.3.2–3), seems to suggest that the crime which Frank commits in this scene is dependent on specific prompting from the devil, articulated by the stage direction '*Dog rubs him*'. Critical interpretation of the significance of the Dog's intervention here ranges from the Dog being seen as no more than an 'accessory after the fact'[19] to Frank being, in effect, possessed by the devil through the Dog's touch.[20] In judging the level of Frank's guilt it is important to remember that, in contrast to the experiences of Sawyer and Cuddy Banks, the Dog remains invisible to him throughout, thus emphasising his ignorance of and vulnerability to the devil's wiles.

Moreover, the Dog plays a dominant role in 3.3, not only forecasting 'an early mischief and a sudden' but also stage-managing Frank's actions and behaviour throughout the scene. This is evident in the provision of the weapon which Frank uses to murder Susan. In the previous scene the dramatists make it clear that Frank, having given up his sword to his servant, is unarmed. Where then does he acquire the knife with which to commit the murder? The quarto text gives no indication, and editors usually supply a clarifying stage direction, '*Draws a knife*', implying that Frank has another weapon about his person.[21] However, this denies the possibility of the Dog's participation allowed for by an unarmed Frank.[22] The governing irony of the scene—that Frank remains *unaware* that the devil is at his shoulder—is heightened when Frank expresses surprise at the ease with which he has managed to tie himself up behind:

> I did not think I could
> Have done so well behind me.   (3.3.72–3)

The audience is aware that this work is accomplished by the Dog as
the quarto stage direction indicates, '*Dog ties him*' (3.3.71.1). In the
Royal Shakespeare Company (RSC) production the Dog also provided the rope for this operation. When reading a play we tend to
pass over such details, but in a production such matters must be
clarified and can produce a crucial impression on an audience.

Other factors add to the impression that the Dog is the effective
stage-manager of this murder scene. Besides wounding himself and
(apparently) tying himself up, Frank further improvises to deflect
suspicion from himself by pointing to Warbeck and Somerton as the
murderers. This scenario is precisely what the Dog has planned and
announced to Cuddy:

> There's a gallant rival loves the maid,
> And likely is to have her. Mark what a mischief,
> Before the morris ends, shall light on him.   (3.1.159–61)

Thus the audience may conclude that Frank's accusation against
Somerton and Warbeck does not stem wholly from his own inven-
tion but is to some degree the direct result of the Dog's control.[23]
The point is reinforced by Cuddy Banks in the scene in which
Warbeck and Somerton are arrested:

> [*Aside*] There's my rival taken up for hangman's meat. Tom told me he
> was about a piece of villainy.   (3.4.69–71)

Significantly the Dog has worked to bring both Frank and Sawyer to
the gallows, and there is a good case for attributing the evil which
afflicts the Edmonton community to his agency. The moment
which, perhaps more than any other in the play, suggests the control
which the Dog exerts is the bizarre one when at the morris dancing,
after bewitching the fiddle, the Dog is described in the quarto SD as
'*playing the morris*' to which the men dance. Although this is one of
the lighter aspects of Tom's villainy, more of a prank than a crime,
the vision for the audience of the morris dance, a symbol of community and good cheer, being presided over and directed by the
devil-dog, is one which symbolises the Dog's control of the play-
world.

However, whilst it may be valid to see Sawyer and Frank as
victims, the text supports a wider interpretative potential. The third
strand of the play's plotting (usually attributed to Rowley) consider-

ably modifies our notion of the power exercised by the Dog in his
manipulation of the characters and the action. The dramatists
mitigate our sense of the devil's control by their presentation of the
relationship between the Clown figure (Cuddy Banks) and the Dog.
Apart from Sawyer, Cuddy is the only character to enjoy a direct
interplay with the devil-dog, and the result of these scenes is to
demonstrate that the devil's power is limited. That Cuddy escapes
from his contact with the Dog unharmed seems entirely appropriate
and indicates that it takes human co-operation to allow evil to
penetrate the community. Cuddy, like other Clown figures in Renaissance Drama (Cokes in Jonson's *Bartholomew Fair*, the Ward in
Middleton's *Women Beware Women*), possesses an innocence which
inoculates him from danger, since, as Alexander Leggatt observes,
'for him a witch is simply his favourite character in the Morris
Dance'.[24] This can be seen in his notion of 'paying' for the Dog's
service, parodying Elizabeth Sawyer's blood-contract:

> Well, you shall have jowls and livers. I have butchers to my friends that
> shall bestow 'em, and I will keep crusts and bones for you, if you'll be a
> kind dog, Tom.   (3.1.134–7)

Cuddy treats the Dog simply as a dog (a pet), and, when he fears
that the Dog's barking will lead to detection and blame, he pretends,
rather like Launce in *Two Gentleman of Verona*, that it was he who
barked, scolding the Dog after the danger has been averted in terms
of endearment which again contrast markedly with those of Elizabeth Sawyer:

> Ningle, you had like to have spoiled all with your bowings. I was glad to
> put 'em off with one of my dog-tricks on a sudden. I am bewitched, little
> cost-me-nought, to love thee—a pox, that morris makes me spit in thy
> mouth.   (4.1.282–6)

Because, as the devil-dog acknowledges, Cuddy has treated the Dog
only as a dog and not as a devil, he remains immune from harm. As
a parting gift Dog gives Cuddy some inside information regarding
the manner in which he inhabits shapes as a familiar, anything from
a dog or cat to a louse or flea. Cuddy's comedic reaction, 'you devils
must have poor thin souls that you can bestow yourselves in such
small bodies', reflects the literalism with which he treats the devil
throughout, and he cannot resist, even at this late stage, trying to
reform the Dog by giving him a reference for an alternative, honest,
vocation:

> if your stomach did better like to serve in some nobleman's, knight's, or gentleman's kitchen, if you could brook the wheel and turn the spit—your labour could not be much . . . Or if you could translate yourself into a lady's arming puppy, there you might lick sweet lips and do many pretty offices.   (5.1.178–86)

Cuddy's comments here reduce the devil to a figure of comic pathos and domesticity, bringing a comic tone to the presentation of the devil, offering the audience an alternative view which undermines the apparent threat and power of forces which elsewhere in the play are tragically destructive. The tone of the Cuddy Banks scenes helps pave the way for the reconciliatory nature of the closure and explains why the quarto's title-page advertises the play as a tragicomedy.

Although the devil is always there to maximise the possibilities for evil, the community of Edmonton itself cannot escape blame for the disasters which occur. Sawyer takes on and repays in full the spite which the community loads on to her; her opening complaint of being made into a 'common sink' is a prescient one. Old Carter's unfair accusation that she bewitched Frank to kill his wife, 'He could never have done't without the devil', earns the characteristically sharp and perceptive rejoinder, 'Who doubts it? But is every devil mine?' (5.3.26–8). Frank, too, may not be culpable in the clear-eyed manner of some of Ford's later tragic heroes, such as Giovanni in 'Tis Pity She's a Whore, who pursue their fates with a Marlovian defiance and lack of restraint. Our overall impression of him is less that of a villain than that of one who is weak enough to try to please everyone—Winnifride, Susan, his father, Old Carter, Katherine—so that he, like Sawyer, is to a degree the victim of the pressures of society.

If an alternative blame to the intervention of the devil is to be located in Edmonton, it lies at the head of the social hierarchy, Sir Arthur Clarington. His manipulation of his servants, Winnifride and Frank, in the opening scene, his expectation that he may continue to cuckold Frank and to use Winnifride as his mistress after their marriage, demonstrate a total neglect of his social responsibilities. This failure attracts Old Carter's bitter censure in the closing moments of the play:

> If luck had served, Sir Arthur, and every man had his due, somebody might have tottered ere this without paying fines, like it as you list.
>
>   (5.3.163–5)

But despite this bitterness, the tone of the ending is one of forgiveness and reconciliation. Carter and Old Thorney are brought together in their grief for the loss of their children; and, most importantly, Winnifride, who in her pregnant and husbandless state is in danger of becoming the next social outcast in the play, is given support by the Carter family, a support which is also solicited from the audience in her epilogue:

> I am a widow still, and must not sort
> A second choice without a good report,
> Which though some widows find, and few deserve,
> Yet I dare not presume, but will not swerve
> From modest hopes. All noble tongues are free;
> The gentle may speak one kind word for me.[25]

STAGE HISTORY

Besides original performances both at court and in the public theatre and revival in the early seventeenth century, *The Witch of Edmonton* has received at least seven British productions in the twentieth century:[26] the Phoenix Society (amateur) at the Lyric, Hammersmith, April 1921, directed by the Rev. Montague Summers; the Old Vic, December 1936, directed by Michel St Denis; The Mermaid Theatre, November 1962, directed by Bernard Miles; the Bristol Old Vic Theatre School (amateur), December 1976, directed by Nat Brenner; the Royal Shakespeare Company at The Other Place, September 1981, directed by Barry Kyle; and again at the Bristol Old Vic Theatre School (amateur), June 1984, directed Peter Symonds; Hen & Chickens, PO Productions, directed by Helen Fry, 2–19 September 1992.

These have included a number of notable actors and performances, particularly in the two most original roles in the play: actresses of the calibre of Sybil Thorndike, Edith Evans ('with the cankerous malice and glimmer of pity the part demands', Williamson) and Miriam Karlin have been attracted to the witch role, the latter notable for her 'powerful sense of emotional isolation';[27] whilst the virtuoso part of the devil-dog has been successfully impersonated by actors such as Russell Thorndike[28] and Miles Anderson, demonstrating the extraordinary power of a role which is at one and the same time compelling both as dog and as symbolic figure. Equally significant in the play's stage history is perhaps the success achieved by actors in smaller roles such as Old Carter and Winnifride, suggesting the overall strength of this play.[29]

Miles Anderson in the RSC production played the Dog as a human figure naked apart from a leather harness which fitted round his neck and loins, and which dangled down behind his back like a tail. He wore dark make-up all over his body, with long black curly hair and bushy eyebrows that managed to suggest both a dog and a ferociously grinning fiend . . . Sometimes he walked on two legs, sometimes crouched, sometimes climbed up walls of the Other Place to observe and intervene.[30]

His first entry on to the stage came startlingly when the Dog emerged from a sack on a wheelbarrow which had been present from the beginning of the scene.[31] The Dog's control of the dramatic action was particularly evident in the scene of Susan's murder where 'the Dog ran round the stage unrolling a length of cord which marked out the perimeter of the field but which also seemed to ensnare Frank and Susan as they came over the stile into the field'.[32] Having provided Frank with the knife to commit the murder, the Dog was also active in intervening to expose Frank in a later scene where 'he lurked under Frank's bed until his black arm leaned out to slip the incriminating bloody knife into Frank's jacket pocket where Katherine could find it'.[33] The effect of playing the Dog as a kind of internal dramatist was to provide a strong link between the three plots of the play and to underline the vulnerability of the whole community to the force of evil.

The keynote of Kyle's production was the establishment of a sense of the everyday life of the community. The set 'with its stiles, barrels, straw, pails, dirty linen and dead birds reminds us that Edmonton was once a rural community'.[34] The cast was frequently engaged in the earlier part of the action in hauling sacks, inspecting their contents, fetching water, churning butter and other such activities so that, as Michael Billington observed, 'we get . . . a strong sense of a tight-knit hypocritical community on which Mother Sawyer seeks reasonable revenge'. Equally convincing in this production was the momentum with which the community identified Sawyer as a scapegoat when, in the second half of the play, the crops have failed and agricultural rituals have been disrupted. As James Fenton commented, the production showed how 'in a society where the failure of a crop may come as an irremediable disaster, a society where the question of survival is most pressing, phenomena such as witch-hunts are a way of responding to a fearful common danger'.[35]

The Witch of Edmonton in performance has seldom failed to provoke appreciative responses from reviewers, and it is to be hoped that future productions will explore further the potential of this rich and absorbing work.

Early modern witchcraft
Sixteenth- and seventeenth-century witchcraft beliefs and practices
are currently areas of extensive research and sharp theoretical debate. The bibliography of the subject is immense. Students who
wish to set *The Witch of Edmonton* within its social context and
broaden their understanding of a complex historical social phenom-
enon might usefully begin with Keith Thomas's *Religion and the
Decline of Magic* (London: Weidenfeld and Nicolson, 1971, repr.
Penguin) which, whilst dauntingly attempting to explore a vast area
of cultural history, sets the agenda for much modern discussion.
More focused discussion of witchcraft may be found in earlier
studies, George Lyman Kittredge, *Witchcraft in Old and New
England* (Cambridge, Mass.: Harvard University Press, 1929) and
C. H. L'Estrange Ewen, *Witch Hunting and Witch Trials* (London:
Kegan Paul, Trench Trübner & Co., 1929), which is especially
useful in its close exploration of court material. Barbara Rosen's
Witchcraft in England, 1558–1618 (Amherst: University of Massachusetts Press, 1991) provides carefully edited reprints of a variety of
witch pamphlets and reports together with wide-ranging and judicious introductory discussion. James Sharpe, *Instruments of Darkness: Witchcraft in England 1550–1750* (Harmondsworth: Penguin,
1996) and Robin Briggs, *Witches and Neighbours: The Social and
Cultural Context of European Witchcraft* (London: Harper Collins,
1996) together provide a survey of recent scholarship.

The play
The Witch of Edmonton has been previously edited as part of collected
editions of the work of John Ford and Thomas Dekker by Henry
Weber, *The Dramatic Works of John Ford*, 2 vols (London, 1811),
William Gifford in *The Dramatic Works of John Ford*, 2 vols (London,
1827; revised by Alexander Dyce, 3 vols, London, 1869), Fredson
Bowers, *The Dramatic Works of Thomas Dekker*, 4 vols (Cambridge:
Cambridge University Press, 1953–61; *Introductions, Notes and Com-
mentaries* by Cyrus Hoy, 4 vols, Cambridge: Cambridge University
Press, 1980). The text has also been edited separately by E. S. Onat
(New York: Garland, 1980), Simon Trussler (London: Methuen,
1983), and Arthur F. Kinney (London: A. & C. Black, New Mer-
maids, 1998). It has also been included in the following anthologies:
Elizabethan and Stuart Plays, ed. C. R. Baskervill, V. B. Heltzel and

A. H. Nethercot, 1935; *Jacobean and Caroline Comedies*, ed. R. G. Lawrence, 1973; *Three Jacobean Witchcraft Plays*, The Revels Plays Companion Library, ed. Peter Corbin and Douglas Sedge (Manchester: Manchester University Press, 1986; reprinted 1998).

A number of studies have considered the play in relation to cultural issues and its treatment of the theme of witchcraft. Michael Hattaway, 'Women and Witchcraft: The Case of *The Witch of Edmonton*', *Trivium* 20 (1985), pp. 49–68, deals with the play's depiction of the social tensions from which witchcraft accusations arose and considers its presentation of the marginal plight of women. Anthony B. Dawson, 'Witchcraft/Bigamy: Cultural Conflict in *The Witch of Edmonton*', *Renaissance Drama* 20 (1989), pp. 77–98, analyses the play's 'dividedness' in revealing the dangers of social change and the attendant ideological strain which this produces. Anthony Harris, 'Instruments of Mischief' in *Night's Black Agents: Witchcraft and Magic in Seventeenth-century English Drama* (Manchester: Manchester University Press, 1980), pp. 90–108, sets the dramatists' treatment of witchcraft in the play in the context of other representations in the early seventeenth century.

Kathleen E. McLuskie in *Dekker and Heywood: Professional Dramatists* (London: Macmillan, 1994) discusses the presentation of Elizabeth Sawyer as a witch in the context of Dekker's interest in transgressing heroines; and in another piece, 'Women and Cultural Production: The Case of Witchcraft', in *Renaissance Dramatists* (Brighton: Harvester Wheatsheaf, 1989), pp. 57–73, the same author attempts to locate the play within witchcraft attitudes of its day and to assess the play's potential as feminist discourse. Diane Purkiss, *The Witch in History: Early Modern and Twentieth-century Representations* (London: Routledge, 1996), attempts to extend a feminist reading of the play in Chapter 9, 'Testimony and Truth', pp. 231–49.

Other plays from the period should be read in order to gain a sense of the sub-genre of domestic tragedy to which *The Witch of Edmonton* relates. Keith Sturgess has edited a collection of three such texts, the anonymous plays *Arden of Faversham* and *A Yorkshire Tragedy* and Heywood's *A Woman Killed with Kindness* in *Three Elizabethan Domestic Tragedies* (Harmondsworth: Penguin, 1969; reissued 1985). Critical works which consider the play within this context include L. L. Brodwin, 'The Domestic Tragedy of Frank Thorney in *The Witch of Edmonton*', *Studies in English Literature* 7 (1967), pp. 311–28, and, in two studies, Viviana Comensoli, *'Household Business': Domestic Plays of Early Modern England* (Toronto, 1996) and 'Witchcraft and Domestic Tragedy in *The Witch of Edmonton*' in *The Politics of Gender in Early Modern Europe*, ed. J. R. Brink, A. P. Coudert and M. C. Horowitz (Kirksville, Mo., 1989). For a wider perspective on the subject of domestic crime see Frances E. Dolan, *Dangerous Familiars: Representations of Domestic Crime in England 1550–1700* (Ithaca and London: Cornell University Press, 1994).

David Atkinson has considered the relationship between the Frank Thorney and Elizabeth Sawyer plots in 'The Two Plots of *The Witch of Edmonton*', *Notes and Queries* 31 (1984), pp. 229–30, and in 'Moral Knowledge and the Double Action of *The Witch of Edmonton*', *Studies in English Literature 1500–1900* (1985), pp. 419–37, he argues that the two plots are bound together by the parallel development of their respective protagonists in their progress towards moral awareness. In his survey, *English Drama: Shakespeare to the Restoration, 1590–1660* (London: Longman, 1988), pp. 221–5, Alexander Leggatt perceptively relates the mixed style of the play to social concerns and community values. Roger Warren appraises the 1981 RSC production of the play directed by Barry Kyle in 'Ford in Performance' in *John Ford: Critical Re-visions*, ed. Michael Neill (Cambridge: Cambridge University Press, 1988), pp. 11–27.

NOTES

1 For discussion of these issues see Robin Briggs, *Witches and Neighbours* (London: Harper Collins, 1996), and James Sharpe, *Instruments of Darkness: Witchcraft in England 1550–1750* (Harmondsworth: Penguin, 1996).

2 See Christina Larner, *Witchcraft and Religion: The Politics of Popular Belief* (Oxford: Oxford University Press, 1984), pp. 71–2.

3 Reprinted by Barbara Rosen in *Witchcraft in England, 1558–1618* (London: Arnold, 1969; repr. Amherst: University of Massachusetts Press, 1991), pp. 190–203.

4 *Daemonologia: A Discourse of Witchcraft, as it was Acted in the Family of Mr Edward Fairfax, of Fuyston, in the County of York etc.*, ed. William Grainge (Harrogate, 1882).

5 E. K. Chambers, *The Elizabethan Stage* (4 vols, Oxford: Oxford University Press, 1923), III.424 (modernised).

6 See Briggs, Chapter VII, 'Men against Women', pp. 257–86.

7 See Appendix for a transcription of this pamphlet.

8 Robert R. Reed, Jnr, *The Occult on the Tudor and Stuart Stage* (Boston, Mass.: Christopher Publishing House, 1965), p. 181.

9 K. M. Briggs, *Pale Hecate's Team* (London: Routledge, 1962), p. 94.

10 See Robin Briggs, pp. 115–21.

11 See Gerald Eades Bentley, *The Profession of Dramatist in Shakespeare's Time* (Princeton: Princeton University Press, 1971), Chapter VIII, pp. 197–234.

12 Quoted by James Sharpe, p. 172.
13 See Keith Thomas, *Religion and the Decline of Magic* (Harmondsworth: Penguin, 1978), Chapter 17, 'Witchcraft and its Social Environment'.
14 See Rosen, p. 29, and George Lyman Kittredge, *Witchcraft in Old and New England* (Cambridge, Mass.: Harvard University Press, 1929), p. 19.
15 See commentary note at 2.1.184.
16 See Appendix, p. 146.
17 See Michael Hattaway, 'Women and Witchcraft: The Case of *The Witch of Edmonton*', *Trivium* 20 (1985), and 4.1.173 note.
18 Of the Mermaid production (1962), a reviewer commented that it was 'the scenes between the old woman and her familiar, locked together in a sad mockery of passion, that stuck deepest in the mind' (*The Times*, 22 November 1962).
19 See *Jacobean and Caroline Comedies*, ed. R. G. Lawrence (London: Dent, 1973), p. 76.
20 See *The Witch of Edmonton, A Critical Edition*, ed. E. S. Onat (New York: Garland, 1980), p. 76.
21 See the following editions: Lawrence; Onat; *Three Jacobean Witchcraft Plays* (Manchester: Manchester University Press, 1986), eds. Peter Corbin and Douglas Sedge; Arthur F. Kinney, ed., New Mermaids (London: A. and C. Black, 1998).
22 See 3.3.24 note.
23 See commentary notes to 3.3.75 and 4.2.68 SD.
24 Alexander Leggatt, *English Drama: Shakespeare to the Restoration, 1590–1660* (London: Longman, 1988), p. 224.
25 In the RSC production of 1981 the Dog appeared at the side of the stage extending a paw towards Winnifride as if to claim her as a future victim. But this interpretation seems inappropriate to the inclusive communal note sounded in the conclusion.
26 See Lisa Cronin, *A Checklist of Professional Productions on the British Stage since 1880 of plays by Tudor and Early Stuart Dramatists*, Renaissance Drama Newsletter Supplement Seven (University of Warwick, 1987), and *Research Opportunities in Renaissance Drama* 25 (1982), 119–21.
27 Kathleen E. McLuskie, *Dekker and Heywood: Professional Dramatists* (London: Macmillan, 1994), p. 147.
28 See *The Nation & The Athenaeum*, 30 April 1921.
29 See *The Times*, 27 April 1921, p. 10; *The Times*, 9 December 1936, p. 12; Ivor Brown, *The Observer*, 13 December 1936.
30 See Roger Warren, 'Ford in Performance', in *John Ford: Critical Revisions*, ed. Michael Neill (Cambridge: Cambridge University Press, 1988), p. 25.
31 See Warren, p. 25.
32 See Warren, p. 25.
33 See Warren, p. 25.
34 Michael Billington, *The Guardian*, 17 September 1981.
35 James Fenton, *The Sunday Times*, 3 October 1982.

The whole argument is this distich.

Forced marriage, murder; murder blood requires.
Reproach, revenge; revenge hell's help desires.

PROLOGUE

The town of Edmonton hath lent the stage
A Devil and a Witch, both in an age.
To make comparisons it were uncivil
Between so even a pair, a Witch and Devil.
But as the year doth with his plenty bring   5
As well a latter as a former spring,
So has this Witch enjoyed the first, and reason
Presumes she may partake the other season.
In acts deserving name, the proverb says,
Once good, and ever; why not so in plays?   10
Why not in this? Since, Gentlemen, we flatter
No expectation, here is mirth and matter.
                                        Master Bird.

---

1. distich] a couplet containing a complete idea.

1. *Edmonton*] a village in Middlesex, seven miles north of London.
2. *A Devil*] a reference to the anonymous play *The Merry Devil of Edmonton* (1602).
5–8.] indicating that the prologue was written for a revival of the play, probably *c.*1635.
12. *mirth and matter*] i.e. both comic and serious material.
13. *Master Bird*] probably the name of the actor who spoke the Prologue. Theophilus Bird, and Ezekiel Fenn, who played Winnifride (see Epilogue), were members of Queen Henrietta's Company in the mid-1630s. Bird first appeared in female roles in the mids-1620s and had graduated to male roles by the mid-1630s.

THE WITCH
OF EDMONTON

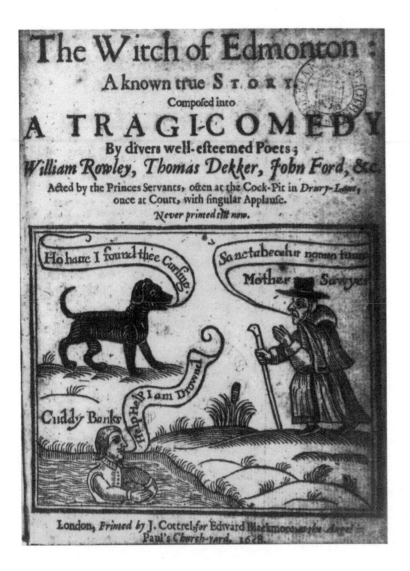

ACTORS' NAMES

SIR ARTHUR CLARINGTON.
OLD THORNEY, *a gentleman.*
OLD CARTER, *a rich yeoman.*
OLD BANKS, *a countryman.*
W. MAGO, } *two countrymen.*
W. HAMLUC, }
Three other Countrymen.
WARBECK, } *suitors to [Old] Carter's daughters.*
SOMERTON, }
FRANK [THORNEY], *Thorney's son.*   10
YOUNG CUDDY BANKS, *the Clown.*
Four Morris Dancers.
OLD RATCLIFFE.
SAWGUT, *an old fiddler.*
POLDAVIS, *a barber's boy.*   15
JUSTICE.
Constable.
Officers.
Servingmen.
DOG, *a Familiar.*   20
A Spirit.

WOMEN

MOTHER [ELIZABETH] SAWYER, *the Witch.*
ANNE, [*Old*] *Ratcliffe's wife.*
SUSAN, } [*Old*] *Carter's daughters.*
KATHERINE, }   25
WINNIFRIDE, *Sir Arthur [Clarington]'s maid.*
[JANE, *a maid.*]

5–6. *W. MAGO/W. HAMLUC*] possibly the names of actors who played minor roles in an early performance. Mago is not referred to elsewhere in the play, but Hamluc enters at 4.1.18 '*with thatch and link*' and is given two brief speeches.

11. *YOUNG CUDDY BANKS*] Cuddy, from 'cudden', ass, a born fool.

15. *POLDAVIS*] a 'ghost' character who, although mentioned by Young Banks at 3.1.67, makes no appearance in the play. The name suggests a Clown, rustic figure or tradesman, since 'poldavy' was a coarse cloth or canvas used for sailcloth and perhaps for rough or cheap clothing. A tailor named Poldavy appears in *Eastward Ho!* (1605).

Act 1

Enter FRANK THORNEY [*and*] WINNIFRIDE *with child.*

Frank Thorney. Come, wench, why here's a business soon
    dispatched.
    Thy heart, I know, is now at ease. Thou needst not
    Fear what the tattling gossips in their cups
    Can speak against thy fame. Thy child shall know
    Who to call dad now.
Winnifride.   You have discharged   5
    The true part of an honest man; I cannot
    Request a fuller satisfaction
    Than you have freely granted. Yet methinks
    'Tis an hard case, being lawful man and wife,
    We should not live together.
Frank Thorney.   Had I failed   10
    In promise of my truth to thee, we must
    Have then been ever sundered. Now the longest
    Of our forbearing either's company
    Is only but to gain a little time
    For our continuing thrift, that so hereafter   15
    The heir that shall be born may not have cause
    To curse his hour of birth, which made him feel
    The misery of beggary and want,
    Two devils that are occasions to enforce
    A shameful end. My plots aim but to keep   20

0.1. with child] i.e. pregnant.

1. *dispatched*] concluded.

3. *gossips*] newsmongers or tattlers, but the primary meaning, 'godparents', might apply here as well.

    in their cups] when drunk.

4. *fame*] reputation.

11. *truth*] troth, pledge.

15. *thrift*] prosperity, success.

My father's love.

Winnifride.   And that will be as difficult
To be preserved, when he shall understand
How you are married, as it will be now,
Should you confess it to him.

Frank Thorney.   Fathers are
Won by degrees, not bluntly, as our masters   25
Or wrongèd friends are. And besides, I'll use
Such dutiful and ready means, that ere
He can have notice of what's passed, th'inheritance,
To which I am born heir, shall be assured.
That done, why, let him know it. If he like it not,   30
Yet he shall have no power in him left
To cross the thriving of it.

Winnifride.   You, who had
The conquest of my maiden love, may easily
Conquer the fears of my distrust. And whither
Must I be hurried?

Frank Thorney.   Prithee do not use   35
A word so much unsuitable to the constant
Affections of thy husband. Thou shalt live
Near Waltham Abbey with thy Uncle Selman.
I have acquainted him with all at large.
He'll use thee kindly. Thou shalt want no pleasures,   40
Nor any other fit supplies whatever
Thou canst in heart desire.

Winnifride.   All these are nothing
Without your company.

Frank Thorney.   Which thou shalt have
Once every month at least.

Winnifride.   Once every month!
Is this to have an husband?

Frank Thorney.   Perhaps oftener;   45

---

32. *cross*] thwart.

33. *conquest of my maiden love*] Winnifride's claim that Frank took her virginity is belied by her admission at lines 160–2.

38. *Waltham Abbey*] near Waltham or Waltham Cross, a village in Hertfordshire, twelve miles north of London, five miles north-east of Edmonton.

39. *large*] length.

40. *use*] treat.
want] lack.

THE WITCH
OF EDMONTON

The Witch of Edmonton :

A known true S т о в у.

Composed into

A TRAGI-COMEDY

By divers well-esteemed Poets;

William Rowley, Thomas Dekker, John Ford, &c.

Acted by the Princes Servants, often at the Cock-Pit in *Drury-Lane*,
once at Court, with singular Applause.

Never printed till now.

Ho haue I found thee Curing.

Sanctabecuhr nomen tiuum

Mother Sawyer

Help Help I am Drownd

Cuddy Banks

London, Printed by J. Cottrel, for Edward Blackmore at the Angel in
Paul's Church-yard. 1658.

ACTORS' NAMES

SIR ARTHUR CLARINGTON.

OLD THORNEY, *a gentleman.*

OLD CARTER, *a rich yeoman.*

OLD BANKS, *a countryman.*

W. MAGO, } *two countrymen.*   5
W. HAMLUC, }

Three other Countrymen.

WARBECK, } *suitors to [Old] Carter's daughters.*
SOMERTON, }

FRANK [THORNEY], *Thorney's son.*   10

YOUNG CUDDY BANKS, *the Clown.*

Four Morris Dancers.

OLD RATCLIFFE.

SAWGUT, *an old fiddler.*

POLDAVIS, *a barber's boy.*   15

JUSTICE.

Constable.

Officers.

Servingmen.

DOG, *a Familiar.*   20

A Spirit.

WOMEN

MOTHER [ELIZABETH] SAWYER, *the Witch.*

ANNE, *[Old] Ratcliffe's wife.*

SUSAN, } *[Old] Carter's daughters.*
KATHERINE, }   25

WINNIFRIDE, *Sir Arthur [Clarington]'s maid.*

[JANE, a maid.]

5–6. W. *MAGO*/W. *HAMLUC*] possibly the names of actors who played minor roles in an early performance. Mago is not referred to elsewhere in the play, but Hamluc enters at 4.1.18 '*with thatch and link*' and is given two brief speeches.

11. *YOUNG CUDDY BANKS*] Cuddy, from 'cudden', ass, a born fool.

15. *POLDAVIS*] a 'ghost' character who, although mentioned by Young Banks at 3.1.67, makes no appearance in the play. The name suggests a Clown, rustic figure or tradesman, since 'poldavy' was a coarse cloth or canvas used for sailcloth and perhaps for rough or cheap clothing. A tailor named Poldavy appears in *Eastward Ho!* (1605).

The whole argument is this distich.

Forced marriage, murder; murder blood requires.
Reproach, revenge; revenge hell's help desires.

PROLOGUE

The town of Edmonton hath lent the stage
A Devil and a Witch, both in an age.
To make comparisons it were uncivil
Between so even a pair, a Witch and Devil.
But as the year doth with his plenty bring   5
As well a latter as a former spring,
So has this Witch enjoyed the first, and reason
Presumes she may partake the other season.
In acts deserving name, the proverb says,
Once good, and ever; why not so in plays?   10
Why not in this? Since, Gentlemen, we flatter
No expectation, here is mirth and matter.
                                        Master Bird.

---

1. distich] a couplet containing a complete idea.

1. *Edmonton*] a village in Middlesex, seven miles north of London.
2. *A Devil*] a reference to the anonymous play *The Merry Devil of Edmonton* (1602).
5–8.] indicating that the prologue was written for a revival of the play, probably *c.*1635.
12. *mirth and matter*] i.e. both comic and serious material.
13. *Master Bird*] probably the name of the actor who spoke the Prologue. Theophilus Bird, and Ezekiel Fenn, who played Winnifride (see Epilogue), were members of Queen Henrietta's Company in the mid-1630s. Bird first appeared in female roles in the mids-1620s and had graduated to male roles by the mid-1630s.

Act 1

Enter FRANK THORNEY [*and*] WINNIFRIDE *with child.*

Frank Thorney. Come, wench, why here's a business soon
    dispatched.
  Thy heart, I know, is now at ease. Thou needst not
  Fear what the tattling gossips in their cups
  Can speak against thy fame. Thy child shall know
  Who to call dad now.
Winnifride.   You have discharged   5
  The true part of an honest man; I cannot
  Request a fuller satisfaction
  Than you have freely granted. Yet methinks
  'Tis an hard case, being lawful man and wife,
  We should not live together.
Frank Thorney.   Had I failed   10
  In promise of my truth to thee, we must
  Have then been ever sundered. Now the longest
  Of our forbearing either's company
  Is only but to gain a little time
  For our continuing thrift, that so hereafter   15
  The heir that shall be born may not have cause
  To curse his hour of birth, which made him feel
  The misery of beggary and want,
  Two devils that are occasions to enforce
  A shameful end. My plots aim but to keep   20

0.1. with child] i.e. pregnant.

1. *dispatched*] concluded.

3. *gossips*] newsmongers or tattlers, but the primary meaning, 'godparents', might apply here as well.

in their cups] when drunk.

4. *fame*] reputation.

11. *truth*] troth, pledge.

15. *thrift*] prosperity, success.

My father's love.
Winnifride.   And that will be as difficult
      To be preserved, when he shall understand
      How you are married, as it will be now,
      Should you confess it to him.
Frank Thorney.   Fathers are
      Won by degrees, not bluntly, as our masters   25
      Or wrongèd friends are. And besides, I'll use
      Such dutiful and ready means, that ere
      He can have notice of what's passed, th'inheritance,
      To which I am born heir, shall be assured.
      That done, why, let him know it. If he like it not,   30
      Yet he shall have no power in him left
      To cross the thriving of it.
Winnifride.   You, who had
      The conquest of my maiden love, may easily
      Conquer the fears of my distrust. And whither
      Must I be hurried?
Frank Thorney.   Prithee do not use   35
      A word so much unsuitable to the constant
      Affections of thy husband. Thou shalt live
      Near Waltham Abbey with thy Uncle Selman.
      I have acquainted him with all at large.
      He'll use thee kindly. Thou shalt want no pleasures,   40
      Nor any other fit supplies whatever
      Thou canst in heart desire.
Winnifride.   All these are nothing
      Without your company.
Frank Thorney.   Which thou shalt have
      Once every month at least.
Winnifride.   Once every month!
      Is this to have an husband?
Frank Thorney.   Perhaps oftener;   45

---

32. *cross*] thwart.

33. *conquest of my maiden love*] Winnifride's claim that Frank took her virginity is belied by her admission at lines 160–2.

38. *Waltham Abbey*] near Waltham or Waltham Cross, a village in Hertfordshire, twelve miles north of London, five miles north-east of Edmonton.

39. *large*] length.

40. *use*] treat.
want] lack.

That's as occasion serves.

Winnifride.   Ay, ay; in case
No other beauty tempt your eye whom you
Like better, I may chance to be remembered,
And see you now and then. Faith, I did hope
You'd not have used me so. 'Tis but my fortune.   50
And yet, if not for my sake, have some pity
Upon the child I go with that's your own.
And, 'less you'll be a cruel-hearted father,
You cannot but remember that.
Heaven knows how—

Frank Thorney.   To quit which fear at once,   55
As by the ceremony late performed,
I plighted thee a faith as free from challenge
As any double thought, once more in hearing
Of heaven and thee, I vow that never henceforth
Disgrace, reproof, lawless affections, threats,   60
Or what can be suggested 'gainst our marriage
Shall cause me falsify that bridal oath
That binds me thine. And, Winnifride, whenever
The wanton heat of youth by subtle baits
Of beauty, or what woman's art can practise,   65
Draw me from only loving thee, let heaven
Inflict upon my life some fearful ruin.
I hope thou dost believe me.

Winnifride.   Swear no more.
I am confirmed, and will resolve to do
What you think most behoveful for us.

Frank Thorney.   Thus then: 70
Make thyself ready; at the furthest house
Upon the green, without the town, your uncle
Expects you. For a little time, farewell.

Winnifride.   Sweet,

---

46. *as occasion serves*] as opportunity arises.

49. *Faith*] in faith. (A mild oath.)

56. *late*] recently.

58. *double*] presumably 'doubly strong'; but a second ironic meaning is also operative: 'deceitful'.

64. *baits*] temptations.

70. *behoveful*] advantageous or necessary.

We shall meet again as soon as thou canst possibly?
Frank Thorney. We shall. One kiss. [*He kisses her.*] Away!
[*Exit* WINNIFRIDE.]

Enter SIR ARTHUR CLARINGTON.

Sir Arthur.   Frank Thorney.
Frank Thorney.   Here, sir.   75
Sir Arthur. Alone? Then must I tell thee in plain terms
   Thou hast wronged thy master's house basely and
     lewdly.
Frank Thorney. Your house, sir?
Sir Arthur.   Yes, sir. If the nimble devil
   That wantoned in your blood rebelled against
   All rules of honest duty, you might, sir,   80
   Have found out some more fitting place than here
   To have built a stews in. All the country whispers
   How shamefully thou hast undone a maid
   Approved for modest life, for civil carriage,
   Till thy prevailing perjuries enticed her   85
   To forfeit shame. Will you be honest yet,
   Make her amends and marry her?
Frank Thorney.   So, sir,
   I might bring both myself and her to beggary,
   And that would be a shame worse than the other.
Sir Arthur. You should have thought on this before, and then   90
   Your reason would have overswayed the passion
   Of your unruly lust. But that you may
   Be left without excuse, to salve the infamy
   Of my disgracèd house, and 'cause you are
   A gentleman and both of you my servants,   95

---

77. *Thou . . . thy*] Sir Arthur addresses Frank with a formality appropriate
to his superior rank.
  82. *stews*] brothel.
  84. *civil carriage*] proper behaviour.
  85. *prevailing perjuries*] i.e. convincing lover's oaths.
  92. *But*] so.
  93. *salve*] lessen, heal.
  95.] It was common practice for the children of the gentry and aristocracy
to be educated by serving in the households of their social superiors.

I'll make the maid a portion.
Frank Thorney.   So you promised me
    Before, in case I married her. I know
    Sir Arthur Clarington deserves the credit
    Report hath lent him, and presume you are
    A debtor to your promise. But upon   100
    What certainty shall I resolve? Excuse me
    For being somewhat rude.
Sir Arthur.   'Tis but reason.
    Well, Frank, what thinkst thou of two hundred pound
    And a continual friend?
Frank Thorney.   Though my poor fortunes
    Might happily prefer me to a choice   105
    Of a far greater portion, yet, to right
    A wrongèd maid and to preserve your favour,
    I am content to accept your proffer.
Sir Arthur.   Art thou?
Frank Thorney. Sir, we shall every day have need to employ
    The use of what you please to give.
Sir Arthur.   Thou shalt have't.   110
Frank Thorney. Then I claim your promise. We are man and
        wife.
Sir Arthur. Already?
Frank Thorney.   And more than so; I have promised her
    Free entertainment in her uncle's house
    Near Waltham Abbey, where she may securely
    Sojourn, till time and my endeavours work   115
    My father's love and liking.
Sir Arthur.   Honest Frank!
Frank Thorney. I hope, sir, you will think I cannot keep her
    Without a daily charge.
Sir Arthur.   As for the money,
    'Tis all thine own, and though I cannot make thee

---

96. *portion*] dowry.
97. *in case*] in the event that.
99. *Report*] rumour.
100–1. *But . . . resolve*] i.e. 'How much money am I assured of?'
102. *rude*] direct.
113. *Free entertainment*] welcome hospitality.
118. *charge*] money to cover expenses.

A present payment, yet thou shalt be sure   120
I will not fail thee.

Frank Thorney.   But our occasions—

Sir Arthur.   Nay, nay,
Talk not of your occasions. Trust my bounty,
It shall not sleep. Hast married her, i'faith, Frank?
'Tis well, 'tis passing well. [*Aside*] Then, Winnifride,
Once more thou art an honest woman. [*To Frank*]
          Frank,   125
Thou hast a jewel. Love her, she'll deserve it.
And when to Waltham?

Frank Thorney.   She is making ready.
Her uncle stays for her.

Sir Arthur.   Most provident speed.
Frank, I will be thy friend, and such a friend.
Thou'lt bring her thither?

Frank Thorney.   Sir, I cannot. Newly   130
My father sent me word I should come to him.

Sir Arthur. Marry; and do. I know thou hast a wit
To handle him.

Frank Thorney.   I have a suit t'ye.

Sir Arthur.   What is't?
Anything, Frank, command it.

Frank Thorney.   That you'll please
By letters to assure my father that   135
I am not married.

Sir Arthur.   How?

Frank Thorney.   Some one or other
Hath certainly informed him that I purposed

---

120. *present*] immediate.

121. *occasions*] needs, requirements.

124. *passing*] very.

126. *deserve*] requite.

128. *stays for*] awaits, expects.

129. *thy*] not in quarto. Gifford's addition improves both sense and metre.

132. *Marry; and do*] i.e. 'Indeed do so'. See note 221 below.

wit] intelligence, skill.

133. *suit*] request.

135. *By letters*] i.e. in writing.

136. *How?*] What do you mean?

To marry Winnifride, on which he threatened
To disinherit me. To prevent it,
Lowly I crave your letters, which he seeing   140
Will credit. And I hope, ere I return,
On such conditions as I'll frame, his lands
Shall be assured.
Sir Arthur.   But what is there to quit
My knowledge of the marriage?
Frank Thorney.   Why, you were not
A witness to it.
Sir Arthur.   I conceive; and then,   145
His land confirmed, thou wilt acquaint him throughly
With all that's passed.
Frank Thorney.   I mean no less.
Sir Arthur.   Provided
I never was made privy to it.
Frank Thorney.   Alas, sir,
Am I a talker?
Sir Arthur.   Draw thyself the letter,
I'll put my hand to it. I commend thy policy.   150
Thou'rt witty, witty Frank. Nay, nay, 'tis fit,
Dispatch it.
Frank Thorney. I shall write effectually.   *Exit.*
Sir Arthur. Go thy way, cuckoo. Have I caught thee, young
          man?
One trouble then is freed. He that will feast
At others' cost must be a bold-faced guest.   155

Enter WINNIFRIDE *in a riding suit.*

---

141. *credit*] believe.

143–4. *But . . . marriage?*] i.e. 'But what can be said to acquit me of any
knowledge of the marriage?' Gifford's emendation '*there* to quit' has been
adopted here, instead of quarto's '*that* to quit', since the latter phrase is
difficult to relate with any precision to Frank's previous comments.

145. *conceive*] understand.

146. *throughly*] thoroughly, fully.

148. *made privy to*] informed of.

150. *policy*] stratagem, crafty device.

153. *cuckoo*] cuckold. Sir Arthur intends to continue his affair with
Winnifride, thereby making Frank a cuckold.

155.1. riding suit] a common riding accessory for women was the safe-
guard, a skirt or half-skirt worn for warmth and to protect the dress from dirt
when travelling.

Win, I have heard the news. All now is safe,
The worst is past. Thy lip, wench. [*He kisses her.*]
    I must bid
Farewell for fashion's sake, but I will visit thee
Suddenly, girl. This was cleanly carried,
Ha, was't not, Win?   160
Winnifride.   Then were my happiness
That I in heart repent I did not bring him
The dower of a virginity. Sir, forgive me,
I have been much to blame. Had not my lewdness
Given way to your immoderate waste of virtue,   165
You had not with such eagerness pursued
The error of your goodness.
Sir Arthur.   Dear, dear Win,
I hug this art of thine. It shows how cleanly
Thou canst beguile, in case occasion serve,
To practise. It becomes thee. Now we share   170
Free scope enough, without control or fear,
To interchange our pleasures. We will surfeit
In our embraces, wench. Come, tell me, when
Wilt thou appoint a meeting?
Winnifride.   What to do?
Sir Arthur. Good, good, to con the lesson of our loves,
Our secret game.

156–7. *Win . . . past*] The quarto's '*Win*' has been taken by some editors
to be a speech-prefix, thus giving her these lines; however it is unlikely that
Winnifride would speak with such a sense of complicity to Sir Arthur given
her subsequent rejection of his advances (ll. 173 ff.). Moreover, the phrase
'the news' seems to apply more obviously to Sir Arthur's recent knowledge
of the marriage than to any matters Winnifride may be presumed to have
learnt off-stage from Frank.

159. *Suddenly*] very soon, without delay.
cleanly carried] neatly done.

160–2. *Then . . . virginity*] i.e. 'I find a measure of happiness in the fact
that I repent that I was not chaste when I married Frank'.

163. *lewdness*] Dyce's conjectural reading 'lewdness' makes much better
sense than quarto's puzzling 'laundress'.

166. *The error . . . goodness*] i.e. 'your warmth of generous emotion'.

169. *To practise*] to scheme or intrigue.

174. *con*] learn by heart.

Winnifride.   Oh, blush to speak it further!   175
    As you're a noble gentleman, forget
    A sin so monstrous. 'Tis not gently done
    To open a cured wound. I know you speak
    For trial. Troth, you need not.
Sir Arthur.   I for trial?
    Not I, by this good sunshine!
Winnifride.   Can you name   180
    That syllable of good and yet not tremble
    To think to what a foul and black intent
    You use it for an oath? Let me resolve you.
    If you appear in any visitation
    That brings not with it pity for the wrongs   185
    Done to abusèd Thorney, my kind husband;
    If you infect mine ear with any breath
    That is not thoroughly perfumed with sighs
    For former deeds of lust, may I be cursed,
    Even in my prayers, when I vouchsafe   190
    To see or hear you! I will change my life
    From a loose whore to a repentant wife.
Sir Arthur. Wilt thou turn monster now? Art not ashamed
    After so many months to be honest at last?
    Away, away! Fie on't!
Winnifride.   My resolution   195
    Is built upon a rock. This very day
    Young Thorney vowed, with oaths not to be doubted,
    That never any change of love should cancel
    The bonds in which we are to either bound
    Of lasting truth. And shall I then, for my part,   200
    Unfile the sacred oath set on record
    In heaven's book? Sir Arthur, do not study
    To add to your lascivious lust the sin
    Of sacrilege; for if you but endeavour

---

179. *For trial*] to test me.
183. *resolve you*] put you out of doubt.
190. *vouchsafe*] allow myself, consent.
194. *honest*] virtuous.
201. *Unfile*] withdraw, delete.
202. *study*] think, attempt.

By any unchaste word to tempt my constancy   205
You strive as much as in you lies to ruin
A temple hallowed to the purity
Of holy marriage. I have said enough.
You may believe me.
Sir Arthur.   Get you to your nunnery,
There freeze in your cold cloister. This is fine!   210
Winnifride. Good angels guide me! Sir, you'll give me leave
To weep and pray for your conversion?
Sir Arthur.   Yes.
Away to Waltham! Pox on your honesty!
Had you no other trick to fool me? Well,
You may want money yet.
Winnifride.   None that I'll send for   215
To you for hire of a damnation.
When I am gone, think on my just complaint:
I was your devil, oh, be you my saint!   *Exit.*
Sir Arthur. Go, go thy ways, as changeable a baggage
As ever cozened knight. I'm glad I'm rid of her.   220
Honest? Marry, hang her! Thorney is my debtor;
I thought to have paid him too, but fools have fortune.
                                                    Exit.

I.2

            Enter OLD THORNEY *and* OLD CARTER.

Old Thorney. You offer, Master Carter, like a gentleman;
I cannot find fault with it, 'tis so fair.
Old Carter. No gentleman I, Master Thorney; spare the

---

209. *Get . . . nunnery*] possibly an echo of Hamlet's advice to Ophelia,
'Get thee to a nunnery' (*Hamlet*, 3.1.119).
210. *cold*] Gifford's emendation 'cold' makes more pointed sense than
quarto's 'old'.
fine] cunning, artful.
216. *for hire . . . damnation*] i.e. to be rewarded with damnation.
219. *Go . . . ways*] i.e. 'Get along with you'.
baggage] strumpet, whore.
220. *cozened*] cheated.
221. *Marry*] an oath; a contraction of 'By Mary' or 'By the Virgin Mary'.
222. *fools have fortune*] Proverbial.

Mastership, call me by my name, John Carter. Master is
a title my father, nor his before him, were acquainted   5
with. Honest Hertfordshire yeomen, such an one am I.
My word and my deed shall be proved one at all times. I
mean to give you no security for the marriage-money.

Old Thorney. How! No security?

Although it need not so long as you live,   10
Yet who is he has surety of his life one hour?
Men, the proverb says, are mortal, else, for my part,
I distrust you not, were the sum double.

Old Carter. Double, treble, more or less, I tell you, Master
Thorney, I'll give no security. Bonds and bills are but   15
tarriers to catch fools and keep lazy knaves busy. My
security shall be present payment. And we here about
Edmonton hold present payment as sure as an alderman's bond in London, Master Thorney.

Old Thorney. I cry you mercy, sir, I understood you not.   20

Old Carter. I like young Frank well, so does my Susan too.
The girl has a fancy to him, which makes me ready in my
purse. There be other suitors within, that make much
noise to little purpose. If Frank love Sue, Sue shall have
none but Frank. 'Tis a mannerly girl, Master Thorney,   25
though but an homely man's daughter. There have worse
faces looked out of black bags, man.

---

6. *Hertfordshire*] county lying north of London.

yeomen] men below the rank of gentleman, who held freehold land. Only
a gentleman might properly by addressed as 'Master'.

8. *security*] bills of promise or IOUs. Dowries were often paid in instal-
ments over a number of years or were tied up until the death of the bride's
father or guardian. Such arrangements were frequently the cause of legal
dispute. Old Carter, however, intends to pay cash down (see ll. 16–17).

11. *surety*] safety, certainty.

12. *Men . . . mortal*] Proverbial, 'All men are mortal'.

16. *tarriers*] hindrances, obstructions.

17. *present*] immediate.

18–19. *alderman's bond*] An alderman was the chief officer of a ward or
district of a city. The aldermen of a city sat on its ruling council.

20. *I cry you mercy*] I beg your pardon.

25. *mannerly*] seemly, decent.

26–7. *There . . . man*] The exact meaning is obscure, but since 'bags' suggests money-bags it seems that Old Carter is suggesting that large dowries
have often procured husbands for ugly brides. Alternatively, 'black bags' may

Old Thorney. You speak your mind freely and honestly. I
marvel my son comes not. I am sure he will be here
sometime today.   30

Old Carter. Today or tomorrow, when he comes he shall be
welcome to bread, beer and beef—yeoman's fare, we
have no kickshaws; full dishes, whole bellyfulls. Should I
diet three days at one of the slender city-suppers, you
might send me to Barber-Surgeons' Hall the fourth day   35
to hang up for an anatomy. Here come they that—

        Enter WARBECK *with* SUSAN, SOMERTON
              with KATHERINE.

How now, girls! Every day play-day with you? Valentine's
day too, all by couples? Thus will young folks do when we
are laid in our graves, Master Thorney. Here's all the care
they take. And how do you find the wenches, gentlemen?   40
Have they any mind to a loose gown and a straight shoe?

---

refer to the black masks worn by society women at balls and banquets, thus
giving Carter's words an edge of social sarcasm, or may be a variation on the
misogynistic slur that if you put a bag over a woman's head and face during
lovemaking it doesn't matter how ugly she is.

  32. *bread . . . fare*] Old Carter's emphasis on the homely fare offered to his
guests shows his pride in his yeoman status and accentuates the range and
richness of the play's social texture.

  33. *kickshaws*] a contemptuous term for fancy dishes; 'a something
French'—the word is a corruption of 'quelque chose'; in contrast to substantial English dishes.

  35. *Barber-Surgeons' Hall*] in Monkswell Street near Cripplegate,
London. The Barber-Surgeons, who were responsible for invasive surgical
procedures, practised their skills by dissecting corpses, especially those of
criminals whose skeletons were sometimes preserved.

  36. *anatomy*] a skeleton; a skeleton retaining its skin, a mummy.

  37–8. *Valentine's day*] traditionally the day (14 February) on which the
birds chose their mates and lovers chose their sweethearts.

  41. *loose gown*] a stylish garment fashionable at this time. An Italian
spectator at Jonson's masque *The Vision of Delight*, given at court, Christmas
1617, provides the following description: 'the dress hangs behind well nigh
from the neck down to the ground, with long close sleeves and no waist.
There are no folds so that any deformity, however monstrous, remains
hidden' (see M. C. Linthicum, *Costume in the Drama of Shakespeare and his
Contemporaries* (1936), p. 183). Besides a jibe at fashionable extravagance,
Old Carter's teasing may carry a bawdy reference, as may 'straight shoe'.

Win 'em and wear 'em. They shall choose for themselves
by my consent.
Warbeck. You speak like a kind father.—Sue, thou hearest
    The liberty that's granted thee. What sayest thou?   45
    Wilt thou be mine?
Susan.   Your what, sir? I dare swear,
    Never your wife.
Warbeck.   Canst thou be so unkind,
    Considering how dearly I affect thee,
    Nay, dote on thy perfections?
Susan.   You are studied
    Too scholar-like in words I understand not.   50
    I am too coarse for such a gallant's love
    As you are.
Warbeck.   By the honour of gentility—
Susan. Good sir, no swearing. Yea and nay with us
    Prevails above all oaths you can invent.
Warbeck. By this white hand of thine—
Susan.   Take a false oath?   55
    Fie, fie! Flatter the wise, fools not regard it,
    And one of these am I.
Warbeck.   Dost thou despise me?
Old Carter. Let 'em talk on, Master Thorney. I know Sue's
    mind. The fly may buzz about the candle; he shall but
    singe his wings when all's done. Frank, Frank is he has   60
    her heart.
Somerton. But shall I live in hope, Kate?
Katherine. Better so than be a desperate man.
Somerton. Perhaps thou thinkst it is thy portion
    I level at? Wert thou as poor in fortunes   65
    As thou art rich in goodness, I would rather

---

42. *Win 'em and wear 'em*] Proverbial, 'Win it and wear it', with a bawdy
implication.

48. *affect*] love.

53. *Yea and nay*] Biblical. Matthew's injunction, 'Let your communica-
tion be, Yea, yea; Nay, nay' (Matt. 5.37), came to be regarded as a particularly earnest oath.

59–60. *The fly . . . done*] Proverbial, 'The fly (moth) that plays too long in
the candle singes its wings at last'.

63. *desperate*] despairing.

65. *level at*] aim for.

Be suitor for the dower of thy virtues
Than twice thy father's whole estate. And, prithee,
Be thou resolvèd so.

Katherine.   Master Somerton,
It is an easy labour to deceive   70
A maid that will believe men's subtle promises,
Yet I conceive of you as worthily
As I presume you do deserve.

Somerton.   Which is
As worthily in loving thee sincerely
As thou art worthy to be so beloved.   75

Katherine. I shall find time to try you.

Somerton.   Do, Kate, do.
And when I fail, may all my joys forsake me.

[Old Carter and Old Thorney converse privately.]

Old Carter. Warbeck and Sue are at it still. I laugh to myself,
Master Thorney, to see how earnestly he beats the bush
while the bird is flown into another's bosom. A very   80
unthrift, Master Thorney, one of the country roaring-
lads. We have such as well as the city, and as arrant rake-
hells as they are, though not so nimble at their prizes of
wit. Sue knows the rascal to an hair's breadth, and will fit
him accordingly.   85

Old Thorney. What is the other gentleman?

Old Carter. One Somerton, the honester man of the two by
five pound in every stone-weight. A civil fellow, he has a
fine convenient estate of land in West Ham, by Essex.
Master Ranges, that dwells by Enfield, sent him hither.   90

---

69. *resolvèd so*] certain of it.

76. *try*] test.

80. *very*] veritable.

81–2. *roaring-lads*] riotous young men.

82–3. *rake-hells*] scoundrels, hell-raisers.

83. *prizes*] contests.

84. *fit*] treat, serve.

88. *five pound . . . stone-weight*] Old Carter expresses his reservations about Warbeck; 'stone-weight' = 14 pounds.

89. *convenient*] a polite reference, equivalent to 'agreeable'.

West Ham] a village four and a half miles from London and sufficiently distant from Edmonton to warrant an explanation of this 'foreigner's' status.

by] near.

90. *Enfield*] a village in Essex eleven miles north of London and three miles north of Edmonton.

He likes Kate well. I may tell you I think she likes him as
well. If they agree, I'll not hinder the match for my part.
But that Warbeck is such another—I use him kindly for
Master Somerton's sake, for he came hither first as a
companion of his. Honest men, Master Thorney, may fall   95
into knaves' company now and then.

Warbeck. Three hundred a year jointure, Sue.

Susan. Where lies it, by sea or by land? I think by sea.

Warbeck. Do I look a captain?

Susan.   Not a whit, sir.
Should all that use the seas be reckoned captains,   100
There's not a ship should have a scullion in her
To keep her clean.

Warbeck.   Do you scorn me, Mistress Susan?
Am I a subject to be jeered at?

Susan.   Neither
Am I a property for you to use
As stale to your fond wanton loose discourse.   105
Pray, sir, be civil.

Warbeck.   Wilt be angry, wasp?

Old Carter. God-a-mercy, Sue! She'll firk him, on my life, if
he fumble with her.

Enter FRANK [THORNEY].

Master Francis Thorney, you are welcome indeed. Your
father expected your coming. How does the right wor-   110
shipful knight, Sir Arthur Clarington, your master?

Frank Thorney. In health this morning. [*To his father*] Sir,
my duty.

Old Thorney.   Now

95–6. *Honest . . . then*] Proverbial; a variation of 'Honest men and knaves
may possibly wear the same cloth'.

97. *Three . . . jointure*] i.e. Warbeck implies that marriage to him would
bring her joint ownership of land to this value together with widow's rights.

98. *by sea*] i.e. in ship's cargoes rather than land, and thus less secure.

101. *scullion*] menial servant.

105. *stale*] decoy, bait, stalking horse, with a secondary meaning of low
prostitute.

fond] foolish.

106. *Wilt . . . wasp*] allusion to the proverb 'As angry as a wasp'.

107. *firk*] beat.

108. *fumble with*] grope sexually.

112. *Sir, my duty*] an expression of respect.

You come as I could wish.

Warbeck.   Frank Thorney, ha!

Susan. You must excuse me.

Frank Thorney.   Virtuous Mistress Susan.
Kind Mistress Katherine.   *Salutes them.*
                          Gentlemen, to both   115
Good time o'th'day.

Somerton.   The like to you.

Warbeck.   'Tis he.
A word, friend. [*To Somerton*] On my life, this is
    the man
Stands fair in crossing Susan's love to me.

Somerton. [*To Warbeck*] I think no less. Be wise, and take
    no notice on't.
He that can win her best deserves her.

Warbeck. [*To Somerton*]   Marry   120
A serving-man? Mew!

Somerton. [*To Warbeck*]   Prithee, friend, no more.

Old Carter. Gentlemen all, there's within a slight dinner
    ready, if you please to taste of it, Master Thorney, Master
    Francis, Master Somerton—Why, girls! What, huswives!
    Will you spend all your forenoon in tittle-tattles? Away!   125
    It's well, i'faith.—Will you go in, gentlemen?

Old Thorney. We'll follow presently. My son and I
Have a few words of business.

Old Carter.   At your pleasure.
                                  Exeunt the rest.

Old Thorney. I think you guess the reason, Frank, for which
I sent for you.

Frank Thorney.   Yes, sir.

Old Thorney.   I need not tell you   130

---

113. *Frank Thorney, ha!*] Some editors have given this as an aside, but
this is unnecessary because Susan's subsequent response suggests that
Warbeck addresses her.

115. SD. Salutes them] greets them, perhaps by kissing them.

118. *Stands . . . crossing*] who is in a good position to thwart.

121. *Mew*] a derisive exclamation.

122. *slight*] light; Old Carter is being self-deprecating here.

124. *Why . . . What*] colloquial expressions of impatience.

huswives] hussies, minxes.

With what a labyrinth of dangers daily
The best part of my whole estate's encumbered.
Nor have I any clew to wind it out
But what occasion proffers me. Wherein
If you should falter I shall have the shame,   135
And you the loss. On these two points rely
Our happiness or ruin. If you marry
With wealthy Carter's daughter, there's a portion
Will free my land, all which I will instate
Upon the marriage to you. Otherwise   140
I must be of necessity enforced
To make a present sale of all, and yet,
For aught I know, live in as poor distress,
Or worse, than now I do. You hear the sum?
I told you thus before. Have you considered on't?   145
Frank Thorney. I have, sir. And however I could wish
To enjoy the benefit of single freedom,
For that I find no disposition in me
To undergo the burden of that care
That marriage brings with it, yet to secure   150
And settle the continuance of your credit,
I humbly yield to be directed by you
In all commands.
Old Thorney.   You have already used
Such thriving protestations to the maid
That she is wholly yours. And, speak the truth,   155
You love her, do you not?
Frank Thorney.   'Twere pity, sir,
I should deceive her.
Old Thorney.   Better you'd been unborn.
But is your love so steady that you mean,
Nay, more, desire to make her your wife?
Frank Thorney.   Else, sir,
It were a wrong not to be righted.
Old Thorney.   True,   160

---

133. *clew*] a ball of thread or yarn which guides or threads a way through
a maze; an allusion to Ariadne's thread which enabled Theseus to escape
from the labyrinth of the Minotaur.

139. *instate*] confer, endow.

It were. And you will marry her?

Frank Thorney.   Heaven prosper it!
I do intend it.

Old Thorney.   Oh, thou art a villain!
A devil like a man! Wherein have I
Offended all the powers so much, to be
Father to such a graceless, godless son?   165

Frank Thorney. To me, sir, this? Oh, my cleft heart!

Old Thorney.   To thee,
Son of my curse. Speak truth and blush, thou monster.
Hast thou not married Winnifride, a maid
Was fellow-servant with thee?

Frank Thorney. [*Aside*]   Some swift spirit
Has blown this news abroad. I must outface it.   170

Old Thorney. D'you study for excuse? Why, all the country
Is full on't.

Frank Thorney. With your licence, 'tis not charitable,
I am sure it is not fatherly, so much
To be o'erswayed with credulous conceit
Of mere impossibilities. But fathers   175
Are privileged to think and talk at pleasure.

Old Thorney. Why, canst thou yet deny thou hast no wife?

Frank Thorney. What do you take me for? An atheist?
One that nor hopes the blessedness of life
Hereafter, neither fears the vengeance due   180
To such as make the marriage-bed an inn
Which travellers day and night,
After a toilsome lodging, leave at pleasure?
Am I become so insensible of losing
The glory of creation's work, my soul?   185
Oh, I have lived too long!

Old Thorney.   Thou hast, dissembler.
Dar'st thou persèver yet, and pull down wrath
As hot as flames of hell to strike thee quick

---

172. *With your licence*] by your leave.
174. *conceit*] imagining.
178. *atheist*] i.e. an unscrupulous person.
179. *nor*] neither.
188. *quick*] alive.

Into the grave of horror? I believe thee not.
Get from my sight!
Frank Thorney.　　　　　Sir, though mine innocence　　　190
　　Needs not a stronger witness than the clearness
　　Of an unperished conscience, yet, for that
　　I was informed how mainly you had been
　　Possessed of this untruth, to quit all scruple
　　Please you peruse this letter. 'Tis to you.　　　　195
　　　　　　　　　　　　　　[*He gives a letter.*]
Old Thorney. From whom?
Frank Thorney.　　　　　Sir Arthur Clarington, my master.
Old Thorney. Well, sir.　　　　　[*He reads the letter.*]
Frank Thorney. [*Aside*] On every side I am distracted,
　　Am waded deeper into mischief
　　Than virtue can avoid. But on I must.
　　Fate leads me, I will follow. [*To him*] There you read　　200
　　What may confirm you.
Old Thorney.　　　　　Yes, and wonder at it.
　　Forgive me, Frank. Credulity abused me.
　　My tears express my joy, and I am sorry
　　I injured innocence.
Frank Thorney.　　　　　Alas! I knew
　　Your rage and grief proceeded from your love　　　205
　　To me. So I conceived it.
Old Thorney.　　　　　My good son.
　　I'll bear with many faults in thee hereafter;
　　Bear thou with mine.
Frank Thorney.　　　　　The peace is soon concluded.

　　　　　Enter OLD CARTER [*and* SUSAN].

Old Carter. Why, Master Thorney, d'ye mean to talk out your
　　dinner? The company attends your coming. What must it　　210
　　be, Master Frank, or son Frank? I am plain Dunstable.

---

192. *for that*] because.
193. *mainly*] strongly.
201. *confirm*] convince.
206. *conceived*] understood.
210. *attends*] awaits.
211. *Dunstable*] honest and straightforward; a reference to the proverb,
'As plain as Dunstable Highway'.

Old Thorney. Son, brother, if your daughter like to have it so.
Frank Thorney. I dare be confident she's not altered
    From what I left her at our parting last.—
    Are you, fair maid?
Susan.   You took too sure possession   215
    Of an engagèd heart.
Frank Thorney.   Which now I challenge.
Old Carter. Marry, and much good may it do thee, son. Take
    her to thee. Get me a brace of boys at a burden, Frank.
    The nursing shall not stand thee in a pennyworth of milk.
    Reach her home and spare not. When's the day?   220
Old Thorney. Tomorrow, if you please. To use ceremony
    Of charge and custom were to little purpose;
    Their loves are married fast enough already.
Old Carter. A good motion. We'll e'en have an household
    dinner, and let the fiddlers go scrape. Let the bride and   225
    bridegroom dance at night together, no matter for the
    guests. Tomorrow, Sue, tomorrow.—Shall's to dinner
    now?
Old Thorney. We are on all sides pleased, I hope.
Susan. Pray heaven I may deserve the blessing sent me!   230
    Now my heart is settled.
Frank Thorney.   So is mine.
Old Carter. Your marriage-money shall be received before

---

212. *Son, brother*] son-in-law, brother-in-law.

216. *challenge*] claim.

218. *brace*] pair.

at a burden] at one birth.

219. *The nursing . . . milk*] i.e. 'The cost of employing a wet-nurse will not fall upon you'.

220. *Reach her home*] i.e. 'Impregnate her thoroughly'.

221–8.] Old Thorney and Old Carter agree to do without the usual trappings of the wedding celebration, e.g. hiring fiddlers and inviting guests, in order to hasten the union. Whereas Old Carter shows his generosity to the young couple, Old Thorney's motives are mercenary.

222. *charge*] expense.

224. *motion*] proposal.

225. *go scrape*] i.e. 'go scrape their fiddles elsewhere, be dispensed with'.

226. *dance at night together*] an allusion to the dance tune 'The Shaking of the Sheets', often used as the basis of a sexual joke.

227. *Shall's*] shall we.

your wedding shoes can be pulled on. Blessing on you
both!

Frank Thorney. [*Aside*] No man can hide his shame from
    heaven that views him.   235
    In vain he flees whose destiny pursues him.   *Exeunt.*

Act 2

Enter ELIZABETH SAWYER *gathering sticks.*

Elizabeth Sawyer. And why on me? Why should the envious
    world
    Throw all their scandalous malice upon me?
    'Cause I am poor, deformed and ignorant,
    And like a bow buckled and bent together
    By some more strong in mischiefs than myself,   5
    Must I for that be made a common sink
    For all the filth and rubbish of men's tongues
    To fall and run into? Some call me witch,
    And, being ignorant of myself, they go
    About to teach me how to be one, urging   10
    That my bad tongue, by their bad usage made so,
    Forspeaks their cattle, doth bewitch their corn,
    Themselves, their servants and their babes at nurse.

Enter OLD BANKS.

1–13.] From the outset Sawyer blames her misfortunes on others, thus directing the audience towards an awareness of scapegoating within the community.

1. *envious*] malicious.

3–4.] Goodcole records that 'Her body was crooked and deformed, even bending together' and later notes that 'she was a very ignorant woman'; see Appendix, pp. 137, 141.

6. *sink*] sewer.

11. *bad tongue*] i.e. scolding, cursing tongue.

12. *Forspeaks*] bewitches, charms.

bewitch . . . corn] either blasting it as it is growing, spoiling it once harvested, or transporting it; see Middleton's *The Witch*:

I'll call forth Hoppo, and her incantation
Can straight destroy the young of all his cattle
Blast vineyards, orchards, meadows, or in one night
Transport his dung, hay, corn, by ricks, whole stacks
Into thine own ground. (1.2.144–7)

This they enforce upon me, and in part
Make me to credit it. And here comes one   15
Of my chief adversaries.

Old Banks. Out, out upon thee, witch!

Elizabeth Sawyer.   Dost call me witch?

Old Banks. I do, witch, I do; and worse I would, knew I a
    name more hateful. What makest thou upon my ground?

Elizabeth Sawyer. Gather a few rotten sticks to warm me.   20

Old Banks. Down with them when I bid thee, quickly. I'll
    make thy bones rattle in thy skin else.

Elizabeth Sawyer. You won't, churl, cut-throat, miser! [*She
    throws down the sticks.*] There they be. Would they stuck
    'cross thy throat, thy bowels, thy maw, thy midriff.   25

Old Banks. Sayest thou me so? Hag, out of my ground!
                                              [*He beats her.*]

Elizabeth Sawyer. Dost strike me, slave, curmudgeon? Now
    thy bones ache, thy joints cramp, and convulsions stretch
    and crack thy sinews!

Old Banks. Cursing, thou hag! Take that and that.   30
                                      [*He beats her and*] *exit.*

Elizabeth Sawyer. Strike, do, and withered may that hand
        and arm
    Whose blows have lamed me drop from the rotten
        trunk.
    Abuse me! Beat me! Call me hag and witch!
    What is the name? Where and by what art learned?
    What spells, what charms or invocations   35
    May the thing called Familiar be purchased?

---

17. *Out . . . thee*] Away with you.

19. *What makest thou?*] i.e. 'What are you doing, up to?'

23. *churl*] miser.

25. *maw*] stomach.

26. *Hag*] (1) an evil spirit, daemon, or infernal being in female form; (2)
a witch; (3) an ugly repulsive old woman, often with implications of vicious-
ness or maliciousness.

27. *curmudgeon*] avaricious churlish fellow; miser.

27–9. *Now . . . sinews*] Sawyer's cursing is reminiscent of the punishments
with which Prospero threatens Caliban in *The Tempest*, 1.2.327–73.

36. *Familiar*] a small, often domestic, animal thought to be provided by
the devil which advised the witch and performed malicious errands, including murder.

Enter YOUNG BANKS *and three or four more*
[Morris Dancers].

Young Banks. A new head for the tabor, and silver tipping for
the pipe! Remember that, and forget not five leash of new
bells.

First Dancer. Double bells! Crooked Lane, ye shall have   40
'em straight in Crooked Lane. Double bells all if it be
possible.

Young Banks. Double bells? Double coxcombs! Trebles, buy
me trebles, all trebles, for our purpose is to be in the
altitudes.   45

Second Dancer. All trebles? Not a mean?

Young Banks. Not one. The morris is so cast we'll have neither mean nor base in our company, fellow Rowland.

Third Dancer. What! Nor a counter?

Young Banks. By no means, no hunting counter. Leave that   50

36.2. *Morris Dancers*] communal folk dancers. Morris dances, often presenting characters from the Robin Hood or the St George legends, were
performed by men dressed in fancy costumes. The dancers were often
accompanied by a hobby-horse (see note 59 below).

37. *head*] skin.

37–8. *tabor . . . pipe*] The tabor (a small hand drum) and the pipe (recorder) were instruments, together with the fiddle, which were most generally favoured to accompany morris dancing.

38. *leash*] set of three; thus five sets of three bells would be attached to the
dancers' legs.

40. *Double*] i.e. sounding an octave lower in pitch.

Crooked Lane] a lane which ran from New Fish Street to St Michael's
Lane, London; the old inn, called the Black Bell, in Fish Street Hill is
possibly alluded to here.

43. *Trebles*] instruments of the highest pitch.

45. *altitudes*] high notes.

46. *mean*] a middle or intermediate part in any harmonised composition.
Young Banks puns on 'mean nor base' at l. 48 in the sense of inferior in rank
or quality.

48. *fellow Rowland*] Although Young Banks refers to the second morris
dancer as Rowland, the quarto text does not identify him in the speech
prefixes.

49. *counter*] i.e. counter-tenor, a pitch higher than tenor. Young Banks
puns on 'hunting counter', i.e. to follow the scent of the game in the reverse
direction; possibly there is also a further quibble on 'Counter' as a name for
the two London debtors' prisons.

to Enville Chase men. All trebles, all in the altitudes.
Now for the disposing of parts in the morris, little or no
labour will serve.

Second Dancer. If you that be minded to follow your leader,
know me, an ancient honour belonging to our house, for   55
a fore-horse in a team and fore-gallant in a morris. My
father's stable is not unfurnished.

Third Dancer. So much for the fore-horse, but how for a good
hobby-horse?

Young Banks. For a hobby-horse? Let me see an almanac. [*He*   60
consults almanac.] Midsummer-moon, let me see ye.
'When the moon's in the full, then's wit in the wane.' No
more. Use your best skill, your morris will suffer an
eclipse.

First Dancer. An eclipse?   65

Young Banks. A strange one.

Second Dancer. Strange?

Young Banks. Yes, and most sudden. Remember the fore-
gallant and forget the hobby-horse. The whole body of
your morris will be darkened. There be of us—but 'tis no   70
matter. Forget the hobby-horse.

---

51. *Enville Chase*] Enfield Chase was a hunting preserve, a dozen miles
north of London, stocked by both Elizabeth and James I.

54. *be minded*] intend.

55. *house*] family.

56. *fore-horse*] leader, lead horse in the team.

fore-gallant] the chief performer or leader in a morris.

59. *hobby-horse*] 'a character common in folk festivals throughout Europe,
and probably a survival of the primitive worshipper clad in the skin of a
sacrificial animal. He rode a wooden or wicker framework shaped like a
horse . . . In England the hobby-horse became a necessary accompaniment
of the Morris dancers and sometimes the Mummers' (Hartnoll).

60–92.] During this sequence Young Banks is fussing and sulking because
of his anxiety to play the hobby-horse himself.

60. *almanac*] a calendar containing astrological information relating to
lucky days, etc.

61. *Midsummer-moon . . . ye*] an allusion to the proverb, 'It is midsummer
moon with you', i.e. a time of lunacy and strange occurrences.

62. *When . . . wane*] Proverbial, 'His wit is in the wane'.

69. *forget the hobby-horse*] a popular catchphrase; Young Banks seems to
be alluding to Puritan disapproval which led to the hobby-horse being
omitted from May-games and festivals.

First Dancer. Cuddy Banks, have you forgot since he paced
    it from Enville Chase to Edmonton? Cuddy, honest
    Cuddy, cast thy stuff.

Young Banks. Suffer may ye all. It shall be known I can take   75
    mine ease as well as another man. Seek your hobby-horse
    where you can get him.

First Dancer. Cuddy, honest Cuddy, we confess and are sorry
    for our neglect.

Second Dancer. The old horse shall have a new bridle.   80

Third Dancer. The caparisons new painted.

Fourth Dancer. The tail repaired.

First Dancer. The snaffle and the bosses new saffroned o'er.
    Kind,—

Second Dancer. Honest,—   85

Third Dancer. Loving, ingenious,—

Fourth Dancer. Affable Cuddy.

Young Banks. To show I am not flint but affable, as you say,
    very well stuffed, a kind of warm dough or puff-paste, I
    relent, I connive, most affable Jack. Let the hobby-horse   90
    provide a strong back. He shall not want a belly when I
    am in 'em.

                    [*He sees Elizabeth Sawyer.*]

    But 'uds me, Mother Sawyer!

First Dancer. The old Witch of Edmonton! If our mirth be not
    crossed—   95

Second Dancer. Bless us, Cuddy, and let her curse her tother
    eye out. What dost now?

72–3. *since . . . Edmonton*] a distance of approximately five miles. An echo
of Will Kemp's famous journey from London to Norwich 'performed in a
daunce' in 1599 and recorded in his *Kemp's Nine Days Wonder* (1600).

74. *cast thy stuff*] don't be offended; literally, quit or throw away your
worthless ideas (*OED* 'stuff' 8b).

81. *caparisons*] trappings for the saddle or harness.

83. *snaffle*] simple form of bridle-bit, having less restraining power than
one provided with a curb.

bosses] metal knobs on each side of a bridle bit.

new saffroned o'er] newly coloured with saffron, i.e. an orange-yellow.

88. *flint*] hard-hearted.

89. *stuffed*] provided for.

puff-paste] fine pastry.

93. *'uds me*] colloquial abbreviation of 'God save me'.

96–7. *her tother eye*] Goodcole records that Elizabeth Sawyer had only one
eye; such deformities were commonly held to be characteristic of witches.

Young Banks. Ungirt, unblessed, says the proverb; but my
    girdle shall serve a riding knot, and a fig for all the witches
    in Christendom! What wouldst thou?   100
First Dancer. The devil cannot abide to be crossed.
Second Dancer. And scorns to come at any man's whistle.
Third Dancer. Away—
Fourth Dancer. With the witch!
All. Away with the Witch of Edmonton!   105
                Ex[*eunt*] *in strange postur*[*es*].
Elizabeth Sawyer. Still vexed! Still tortured! That
    curmudgeon Banks
  Is ground of all my scandal. I am shunned
  And hated like a sickness, made a scorn
  To all degrees and sexes. I have heard old beldams
  Talk of familiars in the shape of mice,   110
  Rats, ferrets, weasels and I wot not what,
  That have appeared and sucked, some say, their blood.
  But by what means they came acquainted with them
  I'm now ignorant. Would some power, good or bad,
  Instruct me which way I might be revenged   115

---

98. *Ungirt, unblessed*] Proverbial; 'Ungirt', unbelted.

98–9. *my girdle . . . a riding knot*] In defiance of the proverb Young Banks
determines to threaten Sawyer by using his belt as a noose, even though by
so doing he risks being unblessed and thus made vulnerable to the devil.

101.] a reference to the popular belief that to cross the devil's path or to
confront him exposed one to his malign influence (cf. *Hamlet*, 1.1.127); there
may also be a second meaning to 'crossed', i.e. to make the sign of the cross.

105.1. in strange postures] It is difficult to be sure how seriously Young
Banks and his companions take the danger of their encounter with Elizabeth
Sawyer. The contortions they perform may indicate some attempt to protect
themselves from her influence or to exit so as to avoid crossing the path of the
devil supposedly accompanying her; or their behaviour may indicate some
form of mockery of her bent posture or even a pretence at their own
bewitchment.

107. *ground*] basis, cause.

109. *degrees*] social classes.

109–12. *I . . . blood*] It was a popular belief that witches fed their familiars
with their own blood either by scratching themselves or by allowing the
familiar to suck blood from the witch's mark, an 'unnatural' mark on the
body which was insensible to pain and which was sometimes thought of as a
teat. See Appendix, pp. 139–40, 143–4.

109. *beldams*] hags, witches.

111. *wot*] know.

Upon this churl, I'd go out of myself
And give this fury leave to dwell within
This ruined cottage ready to fall with age,
Abjure all goodness, be at hate with prayer,
And study curses, imprecations,   120
Blasphemous speeches, oaths, detested oaths,
Or anything that's ill, so I might work
Revenge upon this miser, this black cur
That barks and bites, and sucks the very blood
Of me and of my credit. 'Tis all one   125
To be a witch as to be counted one.
Vengeance, shame, ruin light upon that canker!

Enter DOG.

Dog. Ho! Have I found thee cursing? Now thou art mine own.
Elizabeth Sawyer. Thine? What art thou?
Dog.   He thou hast so often
    Importuned to appear to thee, the devil.
Elizabeth Sawyer.   Bless me! The devil?   130
Dog. Come, do not fear, I love thee much too well
    To hurt or fright thee. If I seem terrible,
    It is to such as hate me. I have found
    Thy love unfeigned, have seen and pitied
    Thy open wrongs, and come, out of my love,   135
    To give thee just revenge against thy foes.
Elizabeth Sawyer. May I believe thee?
Dog.   To confirm't, command me
    Do any mischief unto man or beast,
    And I'll effect it, on condition
    That, uncompelled, thou make a deed of gift   140

116–18. *I'd . . . age*] Sawyer seems to be saying that she would vacate her
own body ('This ruined cottage') in order to allow her vindictive anger free
reign for mischief.

125. *credit*] reputation.

128.] It was thought that the devil needed a favourable opportunity in
order to entrap his victim. Comparison with Marlowe's *Dr Faustus* suggests
Sawyer's relative pettiness and inexperience in blaspheming:

For when we hear one rack the name of God,

Abjure the Scriptures and his Saviour Christ,

We fly in hope to get his glorious soul. (1.3.48–50 A Text)

140. *deed of gift*] Sawyer's contract with the devil-dog closely follows
Goodcole's pamphlet (see Appendix). It would appear from the text that she

Of soul and body to me.
Elizabeth Sawyer.   Out, alas!
    My soul and body?
Dog.   And that instantly,
    And seal it with thy blood. If thou deniest
    I'll tear thy body in a thousand pieces.
Elizabeth Sawyer. I know not where to seek relief. But shall I,   145
    After such covenants sealed, see full revenge
    On all that wrong me?
Dog.   Ha, ha! Silly woman!
    The devil is no liar to such as he loves.
    Didst ever know or hear the devil a liar
    To such as he affects?   150
Elizabeth Sawyer. Then I am thine, at least so much of me
    As I can call mine own.
Dog.   Equivocations?
    Art mine or no? Speak or I'll tear—
Elizabeth Sawyer.   All thine.
Dog. Seal't with thy blood.
                            Sucks her arm; thunder and lightning.
                            See, now I dare call thee mine.
    For proof, command me. Instantly I'll run   155
    To any mischief; goodness can I none.
Elizabeth Sawyer. And I desire as little. There's an old churl,
    One Banks—
Dog. That wronged thee. He lamed thee, called thee witch.
Elizabeth Sawyer. The same; first upon him I'd be revenged.

---

gives both body and soul to the devil and is therefore damned. However,
some writers on witchcraft argued that such compacts were invalid since one
could not renounce the benefits of baptism. In Marlowe's play Faustus is
consigned to hell because of his own fear and despair in refusing to seek
Christ's mercy (*Dr Faustus*, 5.2 A Text).

141. *Out*] an expression of dismay.

150. *affects*] loves.

154. *SD*] Gifford's expanded SD—'*She pricks her arm, which he sucks*'—
offers a more explicit indication of Sawyer's eagerness for the pact. In view
of lines 123–5, which seem to operate as an ironical pre-echo of the business
enacted here, a more credible piece of stage business would be for Dog to
bite Elizabeth's proffered arm before sucking her blood. In the 1981 RSC
production Elizabeth Sawyer took a positive role in order to complete the
contract with the devil by scratching her chest to let blood from the wounds
inflicted earlier by Old Banks.

Dog. Thou shalt. Do but name how.

Elizabeth Sawyer.   Go touch his life.   160

Dog. I cannot.

Elizabeth Sawyer. Hast thou not vowed? Go kill the slave.

Dog. I wonnot.

Elizabeth Sawyer. I'll cancel then my gift.

Dog.   Ha, ha!

Elizabeth Sawyer.   Dost laugh?
  Why wilt not kill him?

Dog.   Fool, because I cannot.
  Though we have power, know it is circumscribed   165
  And tied in limits. Though he be curst to thee,
  Yet of himself he is loving to the world
  And charitable to the poor. Now men
  That, as he, love goodness, though in smallest measure,
  Live without compass of our reach. His cattle   170
  And corn I'll kill and mildew, but his life,
  Until I take him as I late found thee,
  Cursing and swearing, I have no power to touch.

Elizabeth Sawyer. Work on his corn and cattle then.

Dog.   I shall.
  The Witch of Edmonton shall see his fall   175
  If she at least put credit in my power,
  And in mine only, make orisons to me,
  And none but me.

Elizabeth Sawyer.   Say how, and in what manner.

Dog. I'll tell thee. When thou wishest ill,

---

160. *touch his life*] kill him.

162. *wonnot*] will not.

164. *because I cannot*] The devil's power to injure the faithful was held to be very limited; cf. Mephistopheles's reply to Faustus's command to torment the Old Man:

  His faith is great; I cannot touch his soul;
  But what I may afflict his body with
  I will attempt, which is but little worth. (*Dr Faustus*, 5.1.79–81 A Text)

166. *curst*] malignant, perversely disagreeable (*OED* 4). The quarto spelling 'cursed' might suggest an alternative meaning 'deserving a curse, damnable'.

170. *without compass of*] outside the compass of.

172. *late*] recently.

177. *orisons*] prayers.

Corn, man or beast would spoil or kill,   180
Turn thy back against the sun
And mumble this short orison:
If thou to death or shame pursue 'em,
Sanctibicetur nomen tuum.
Elizabeth Sawyer. If thou to death or shame pursue 'em   185
Sanctibecetur nomen tuum.
Dog. Perfect. Farewell. Our first-made promises
We'll put in execution against Banks.   *Exit.*
Elizabeth Sawyer. Contaminetur nomen tuum. I'm an expert
scholar,
Speak Latin, or I know not well what language,   190
As well as the best of 'em. But who comes here?

Enter YOUNG BANKS.

The son of my worst foe. *To death pursue 'em*
Et sanctabecetur nomen tuum.
Young Banks. [Aside] What's that she mumbles? The devil's
pater noster? Would it were else!—Mother Sawyer, good   195
morrow.
Elizabeth Sawyer. Ill morrow to thee, and all the world that
flout a poor old woman. *To death pursue 'em,*
And sanctabacetur nomen tuum.
Young Banks. Nay, good Gammer Sawyer, whate'er it please   200

184.] a parody of the Lord's Prayer, 'Hallowed be thy name'; being the
devil, the Dog appears unable to use the correct term, *sanctificetur.* The
quarto text's varied spelling of 'sanctibicetur' (used six times with six different spellings) in Sawyer's attempts to recite and implement this curse is
retained here, since the variations seem to show her insecure grasp of the
Latin charm which the Dog has attempted to teach her. In Goodcole's
pamphlet Sawyer confirms such ignorance when she claims that she was not
taught the Latin words by anyone but 'by the Devil alone; neither do I
understand the meaning of these words nor can speak any more Latin words'
(see Appendix, p. 146). Lawrence suggests another explanation for the varied
spelling: a desire to avoid an accusation of blasphemy on the part of the
printer.

189. Contaminetur] polluted, be defiled. Interestingly, Sawyer uses a correct Latin term here which she has not been taught but which ironically is an
insult appropriate to the devil.

195. pater noster] 'Our Father', i.e. the Lord's Prayer.

200. *Gammer*] a rustic title for an old woman, corresponding to 'gaffer'
for a man.

my father to call you, I know you are—
Elizabeth Sawyer. A witch.
Young Banks. A witch? Would you were else, i'faith!
Elizabeth Sawyer. Your father knows I am by this.
Young Banks. I would he did.   205
Elizabeth Sawyer. And so in time may you.
Young Banks. I would I might else. But, witch or no witch,
     you are a motherly woman, and though my father be a
     kind of God-bless-us, as they say, I have an earnest suit to
     you. And if you'll be so kind to ka me one good turn, I'll   210
     be so courteous as to kob you another.
Elizabeth Sawyer. What's that? To spurn, beat me and call me
     witch, as your kind father doth?
Young Banks. My father? I am ashamed to own him. If he has
     hurt the head of thy credit there's money to buy thee a   215
     plaster. [*He gives her money.*] And a small courtesy I
     would require at thy hands.
Elizabeth Sawyer. You seem a good young man, [*Aside*] and
     I must dissemble the better to accomplish my revenge.
     [*To him*] But for this silver, what wouldst have me do?   220
     Bewitch thee?
Young Banks. No, by no means, I am bewitched already. I
     would have thee so good as to unwitch me, or witch
     another with me for company.
Elizabeth Sawyer. I understand thee not. Be plain, my son.   225
Young Banks. As a pike-staff, mother. You know Kate Carter?

---

204. *by this*] i.e. by this time. Sawyer assumes that the devil will, by now,
have completed his work against Banks.

208-9. *a . . . God-bless-us*] obscure, though probably a euphemism, perhaps meaning a person addicted to praying.

210-11. *ka me . . . kob you*] i.e. 'scratch my back, I'll scratch yours'. A
variation of the proverb 'Ka me, ka thee'.

212. *spurn*] kick.

214. *own*] acknowledge.

215. *head . . . credit*] i.e. Mother Sawyer's ability to borrow money; but
also 'head' in its physical sense, since Old Banks may have so injured her that
she needs a medicinal plaster for her wounds.

223-4. *unwitch . . . another*] It was believed that love could be induced by
witchcraft; in Middleton's *The Witch* Almachildes seeks out the witches for
such a charm.

226. *as a pike-staff*] Proverbial, 'As plain as a pikestaff'.

Elizabeth Sawyer. The wealthy yeoman's daughter. What of
    her?

Young Banks. That same party hath bewitched me.

Elizabeth Sawyer. Bewitched thee?   230

Young Banks. Bewitched me, *hisce auribus.* I saw a little devil
    fly out of her eye like a burbolt, which sticks at this hour
    up to the feathers in my heart. Now my request is to send
    one of thy what-d'ye-call-'ems, either to pluck that out,
    or stick another as fast in hers. Do, and here's my hand,   235
    I am thine for three lives.

Elizabeth Sawyer. [*Aside*] We shall have sport. [*To him*] Thou
    art in love with her?

Young Banks. Up to the very hilts, mother.

Elizabeth Sawyer. And thou'dst have me make her love thee   240
    too?

Young Banks. [*Aside*] I think she'll prove a witch in earnest.
    [*To her*] Yes, I could find in my heart to strike her three
    quarters deep in love with me too.

Elizabeth Sawyer. But dost thou think that I can do't, and I   245
    alone?

Young Banks. Truly, Mother Witch, I do verily believe so
    and, when I see it done, I shall be half persuaded so too.

Elizabeth Sawyer. It's enough. What art can do, be sure of.
    Turn to the west, and whatsoe'er thou hearest or seest,   250
    stand silent and be not afraid.

      [*Young Banks turns his back upon her.*] *She stamps.*
        Enter the DOG; *he fawns and leaps upon her.*

Young Banks. Afraid, Mother Witch? Turn my face to the
    west? I said I should always have a back-friend of her, and
    now it's out. An her little devil should be hungry, come

---

    231. hisce auribus] by these ears.

    232. *burbolt*] bird-bolt; a blunt-headed arrow used for shooting birds.

    236. *for three lives*] an allusion to legal terminology for land or property
held for the lives of three persons.

    239. *hilts*] the handle of a sword or dagger.

    253. *back-friend*] a backer or supporter, but also, ironically, a pretended
or false friend.

    254. *it's out*] it has turned out to be the case.

    An] if, supposing.

sneaking behind me like a cowardly catchpole and clap   255
his talons on my haunches! 'Tis woundy cold, sure. I
dudder and shake like an aspen-leaf, every joint of me.

Elizabeth Sawyer. *To scandal and disgrace pursue 'em*
Et sanctabicetur nomen tuum.
How now, my son, how is't?   *Exit* DOG.   260

Young Banks. Scarce in a clean life, Mother Witch. But did
your goblin and you spout Latin together?

Elizabeth Sawyer. A kind of charm I work by. Didst thou hear
me?

Young Banks. I heard I know not the devil what mumble in a   265
scurvy base tone, like a drum that had taken cold in the
head the last muster. Very comfortable words. What were
they? And who taught them you?

Elizabeth Sawyer. A great learned man.

Young Banks. Learned man! Learned devil it was as soon! But   270
what, what comfortable news about the party?

Elizabeth Sawyer. Who? Kate Carter? I'll tell thee. Thou
knowst the stile at the west end of thy father's peas-field.
Be there tomorrow night after sunset, and the first live
thing thou seest be sure to follow, and that shall bring   275
thee to thy love.

Young Banks. In the peas-field? Has she a mind to codlings
already? The first living thing I meet, you say, shall bring
me to her?

Elizabeth Sawyer. To a sight of her, I mean. She will seem   280
wantonly coy and flee thee, but follow her close and

---

255. *catchpole*] sheriff's officer or sergeant.

256. *talons*] claws; associated with law officers in Renaissance drama.

woundy] i.e. extremely, excessively.

257. *dudder*] shudder or shiver.

shake . . . aspen-leaf] Proverbial, 'He trembles (quakes, shakes) like an
aspen leaf'.

262. *goblin*] a mischievous and ugly demon.

Latin] Ghosts and devils were commonly thought to converse in Latin.

265. *the devil what*] what devilish.

267. *muster*] assembling of troops for inspection, etc.

273. *peas-field*] reputedly a favourite place for sexual assignations.

277. *codlings*] The context would suggest green or young peas, but
'codlings' more usually means immature or half-grown apples; used here to
suggest a bawdy quibble on 'codling' meaning 'scrotum'. There may also be
a pun on 'cuddlings'.

boldly. Do but embrace her in thy arms once and she is
thine own.

Young Banks. At the stile at the west end of my father's peas-
land, the first live thing I see, follow and embrace her and   285
she shall be thine. Nay, an I come to embracing once she
shall be mine. I'll go near to make at eaglet else.   *Exit.*

Elizabeth Sawyer. A ball well bandied! Now the set's half won.
The father's wrong I'll wreak upon the son.   *Exit.*

2.2

Enter [OLD] CARTER, WARBECK [*and*] SOMERTON.

Old Carter. How now, gentlemen! Cloudy? I know, Master
Warbeck, you are in a fog about my daughter's marriage.

Warbeck. And can you blame me, sir?

Old Carter. Nor you me justly. Wedding and hanging are tied
up both in a proverb, and destiny is the juggler that unties   5
the knot. My hope is you are reserved to a richer fortune
than my poor daughter.

Warbeck. However, your promise—

Old Carter. Is a kind of debt, I confess it.

Warbeck. Which honest men should pay.   10

Old Carter. Yet some gentlemen break in that point now and
then, by your leave, sir.

Somerton. I confess thou hast had a little wrong in the wench,
but patience is the only salve to cure it. Since Thorney

---

287. *make*] win.

at eaglet] probably an obscure card or dice game, so that Young Banks is
saying that he'll assuage his sorrows if he fails to possess Kate by winning at
cards or dice. Some editors have emended the text in various ways: (1) 'an
eaglet', suggesting how the young eagle ventures forth on expeditions under
the guidance of a parent; (2) 'a taglet', suggesting that he would cling to Kate
like a tendril.

288. *bandied*] struck to and fro.

set's] i.e. a set number of games, as in tennis or cards.

1. *Cloudy*] gloomy, sullen.

2. *in a fog*] at a loss to know what to do.

4–6. *Wedding . . . knot*] Proverbial, 'Wedding and hanging go by destiny'.
Old Carter's comments turn out to be ironically appropriate.

8–9. *promise . . . debt*] Proverbial, 'Promise is debt'.

has won the wench, he has most reason to wear her.   15

Warbeck. Love in this kind admits no reason to wear her.

Old Carter. Then love's a fool, and what wise man will take
exception?

Somerton. Come, frolic, Ned. Were every man master of his
own fortune, Fate might pick straws and Destiny go a-   20
wool-gathering.

Warbeck. You hold yours in a string, though. 'Tis well, but if
there be any equity, look thou to meet the like usage ere
long.

Somerton. In my love to her sister Katherine? Indeed, they are   25
a pair of arrows drawn out of one quiver and should fly at
an even length. If she do run after her sister—

Warbeck. Look for the same mercy at my hands as I have
received at thine.

Somerton. She'll keep a surer compass. I have too strong a   30
confidence to mistrust her.

Warbeck. And that confidence is a wind that has blown many
a married man ashore at Cuckold's Haven, I can tell you.
I wish yours more prosperous, though.

Old Carter. Whate'er you wish, I'll master my promise to him.   35

Warbeck. Yes, as you did to me.

Old Carter. No more of that, if you love me. But for the more
assurance, the next offered occasion shall consummate
the marriage, and that once sealed—

Enter YOUNG [FRANK] THORNEY *and* SUSAN.

---

15. *wear*] possess.

17. *love's a fool*] Proverbial, 'Love is without reason'.

19. *frolic*] be merry.

19–21. *Were . . . a-wool-gathering*] Probably proverbial; 'pick straws', fuss
over detail.

22. *You . . . string*] Proverbial, 'To have the world (fortune) in a string'.

27. *run*] take.

30. *compass*] the curved path described by an arrow.

33. *Cuckold's Haven*] a point on the Surrey side of the Thames about a
mile below Rotherhithe Church. It was traditional on St Luke's Day, 18
October, for a butcher of Eastcheap to commemorate King John's cuckold-
ing of a miller by erecting a pair of horns on a pole there. The spot was
renowned for storms; see Jonson, Chapman and Marston's *Eastward Ho!*
(1605), 4.1 (Revels ed.).

35. *master*] keep.

Somerton. Leave the manage of the rest to my care. But see,   40
    the bridegroom and bride come, the new pair of Sheffield
    knives fitted both to one sheath.
Warbeck. The sheath might have been better fitted if some-
    body had their due. But—
Somerton. No harsh language, if thou lovest me. Frank   45
    Thorney has done—
Warbeck. No more than I, or thou, or any man, things so
    standing, would have attempted.
Somerton. Good-morrow, Master Bridegroom.
Warbeck.   Come, give thee joy.
    Mayst thou live long and happy in thy fair choice.   50
Frank Thorney. I thank ye, gentlemen.
    Kind Master Warbeck, I find you loving.
Warbeck. Thorney, that creature—much good do thee with
    her—
    Virtue and beauty hold fair mixture in her.
    She's rich, no doubt, in both. Yet were she fairer,   55
    Thou art right worthy of her. Love her, Thorney;
    'Tis nobleness in thee, in her but duty.
    The match is fair and equal; the success
    I leave to censure. Farewell, Mistress Bride:
    Till now elected, thy old scorn deride.   *Exit.*   60
Somerton. Good Master Thorney.   [*Exit.*]

41–2. *Sheffield knives*] a common wedding gift, being a symbol of twofold
union; Sheffield was already famous for cutlery.

45–6.] This speech is given to Carter in the quarto text, but Warbeck's
reply and his use of the familiar address 'thou' at l. 47 are sufficient to
indicate that the speech would be inappropriate for Old Carter, who uses the
formal 'you' in addressing the suitors.

47–8. *things so standing*] in the circumstances (with a bawdy quibble on
'standing').

59. *censure*] judgement, opinion; but also implying adverse judgement or
unfavourable opinion.

60.] Warbeck's meaning is unclear. Gifford believed that the line is addressed to Frank 'and conveys some obscure hint of a knowledge of his
former connection with Winnifride' and that it is evident from what follows
that it awakens his conscience. It seems more likely that the line is addressed
to Susan since she has treated Warbeck scornfully in 1.2.46–57. The general
sense may be that since Susan is now a bride she should give up her scornful
attitude to Warbeck. Weber's emendation 'new elected' does not resolve the
problem.

Old Carter. Nay, you shall not part till you see the barrels run
    a-tilt, gentlemen.   *Exit.*
Susan. Why change you your face, sweetheart?
Frank Thorney.   Who? I?
    For nothing.
Susan.   Dear, say not so. A spirit of your   65
    Constancy cannot endure this change for nothing.
    I have observed strange variations in you.
Frank Thorney. In me?
Susan.   In you, sir. Awake! You seem to dream,
    And in your sleep you utter sudden and
    Distracted accents, like one at enmity   70
    With peace. Dear loving husband, if I may dare
    To challenge any interest in you,
    Give me the reason fully. You may trust
    My breast as safely as your own.
Frank Thorney.   With what?
    You half amaze me. Prithee–
Susan.   Come, you shall not,   75
    Indeed, you shall not shut me from partaking
    The least dislike that grieves you. I am all yours.
Frank Thorney. And I all thine.
Susan.   You are not, if you keep
    The least grief from me; but I find the cause:
    It grew from me.
Frank Thorney.   From you?
Susan.   From some distaste   80
    In me or my behaviour. You are not kind
    In the concealment. 'Las, sir, I am young,
    Silly and plain; more, strange to those contents

    62–3. *till . . . run a-tilt*] i.e. 'until the barrels are empty and the wedding
guests have had their fill'. Some editors have seen the line as a reference to
running at the quintain, a popular imitation of jousting or running at the
ring, in which a barrel was used as the target, but this seems to be inappropriate as Old Carter has cancelled elaborate entertainment and ceremony in
hastening the wedding; see 1.2.224 ff.
    67. *variations*] changes of expression and behaviour.
    70. *accents*] words.
    72. *challenge*] claim.
    83. *Silly*] innocent, simple.
    more, strange to] i.e. moreover, unfamiliar with.
    contents] contentments.

A wife should offer. Say but in what I fail,
I'll study satisfaction.

Frank Thorney.   Come, in nothing.   85

Susan. I know I do. Knew I as well in what,
    You should not long be sullen. Prithee, love,
    If I have been immodest or too bold,
    Speak't in a frown; if peevishly too nice,
    Show't in a smile. Thy liking is the glass   90
    By which I'll habit my behaviour.

Frank Thorney. Wherefore dost weep now?

Susan.   You, sweet, have the power
    To make me passionate as an April day;
    Now smile, then weep; now pale, then crimson red.
    You are the powerful moon of my blood's sea,   95
    To make it ebb or flow into my face
    As your looks change.

Frank Thorney.   Change thy conceit, I prithee.
    Thou art all perfection. Diana herself
    Swells in thy thoughts and moderates thy beauty.
    Within thy left eye amorous Cupid sits   100
    Feathering love-shafts, whose golden heads he dipped
    In thy chaste breast. In the other lies
    Blushing Adonis scarfed in modesties.

---

85. *study satisfaction*] endeavour to give satisfaction.

89. *nice*] shy, coy.

90. *glass*] mirror.

91. *habit*] fashion.

93. *passionate*] susceptible to swift changes of mood.

97. *conceit*] fanciful notion or opinion.

98–107.] Frank's elevated and artificial rhetoric, which presents Susan in terms derived from emblem books, is uncharacteristic of his normal register and suggests his deep unease when confronted by Susan's pointed questions about his state of mind.

98. *Diana*] the moon goddess, patroness of chastity.

99. *moderates*] presides over.

100. *Cupid*] the god of love. He was said to carry arrows of gold to cause love, and arrows of lead to repel it.

102. *In thy*] The quarto text has a dash before 'In', possibly indicating that the compositor was unable to decipher the first word in the manuscript; the likelihood that a word is missing is also suggested by the deficiency of the metrical line.

103. *Blushing Adonis*] a handsome youth beloved and pursued immodestly by the goddess Venus; see Shakespeare's poem *Venus and Adonis*.

And still as wanton Cupid blows love-fires,
Adonis quenches out unchaste desires.   105
And from these two I briefly do imply
A perfect emblem of thy modesty.
Then, prithee, dear, maintain no more dispute,
For when thou speakst, it's fit all tongues be mute.
Susan. Come, come, those golden strings of flattery   110
    Shall not tie up my speech, sir. I must know
    The ground of your disturbance.
Frank Thorney.   Then look here,
    For here, here is the fen in which this Hydra
    Of discontent grows rank.
Susan.   Heaven shield it! Where?
Frank Thorney. In mine own bosom, here the cause has root.   115
    The poisoned leeches twist about my heart,
    And will, I hope, confound me.
Susan.   You speak riddles.
Frank Thorney. Take't plainly then. 'Twas told me by a
        woman,
    Known and approved in palmistry,
    I should have two wives.
Susan.   Two wives? Sir, I take it   120
    Exceeding likely. But let not conceit hurt you.
    You are afraid to bury me?
Frank Thorney.   No, no, my Winnifride.
Susan. How say you? Winnifride? You forget me.
Frank Thorney. No, I forget myself, Susan.
Susan.   In what?
Frank Thorney. Talking of wives, I pretend Winnifride,   125

---

105. *quenches out*] extinguishes.

113. *Hydra*] the fabled many-headed snake who lived in the marshes and
whose heads grew as they were cut off.

116. *poisoned leeches*] 'leeches', aquatic blood-sucking worms used for
medicinal purposes into the twentieth century. Susan's bafflement is understandable in view of the contradiction of 'poisoned' leeches harming rather
than curing a patient.

117. *confound*] destroy.

121. *conceit*] a fanciful notion. Susan thinks that Frank merely fears that
he will outlive her and then marry again. Women often died in childbirth.

125. *pretend*] Frank's meaning is ambiguous since 'pretend' can mean
both 'use as a pretext' and 'lay claim to'.

A maid that at my mother's waited on me
Before thyself.
Susan.   I hope, sir, she may live
To take my place. But why should all this move you?
Frank Thorney. [*Aside*] The poor girl! She has't before thee,
And that's the fiend torments me.
Susan.   Yet why should this   130
Raise mutiny within you? Such presages
Prove often false, or say it should be true?
Frank Thorney. That I should have another wife?
Susan.   Yes, many;
If they be good, the better.
Frank Thorney.   Never any equal
To thee in goodness.
Susan.   Sir, I could wish I were   135
Much better for you. Yet if I knew your fate
Ordained you for another, I could wish,
So well I love you and your hopeful pleasure,
Me in my grave, and my poor virtues added
To my successor.
Frank Thorney.   Prithee, prithee, talk not   140
Of death or graves. Thou art so rare a goodness
As death would rather put itself to death
Than murder thee. But we, as all things else,
Are mutable and changing.
Susan.   Yet you still move
In your first sphere of discontent. Sweet, chase   145

129–30.] Editors have encountered considerable difficulty with these lines
and some have marked part or all of this speech as an aside. It seems unlikely
that Susan hears Frank's words in view of her immediate response. In
addition it is unclear who Frank means by 'The poor girl', Susan or
Winnifride, and how we may interpret 'She has't before thee'. If the speech
is to be given as an aside, Frank has the opportunity to express his private
feelings to the audience repressed until now. Two issues concern him in his
bigamous situation: his guilt at his prior commitment to Winnifride and his
further guilt prompted by Susan's innocence and generosity of spirit. In the
circumstances with Susan onstage it seems likely that an audience would take
'The poor girl' to refer to Susan, and 'She has't before thee' to refer to the
prior marriage to Winnifride.

129. *She . . . thee*] i.e. 'She has my marriage vow before you'.

145. *sphere*] orbit of a planet from which it is impossible to escape. Susan
recognises that Frank remains locked into his own distress.

Those clouds of sorrow, and shine clearly on me.
Frank Thorney. At my return I will.
Susan.   Return? Ah me!
   Will you then leave me?
Frank Thorney.   For a time I must.
   But how? As birds their young, or loving bees
   Their hives, to fetch home richer dainties.
Susan.   Leave me?   150
   Now has my fear met its effect. You shall not,
   Cost it my life, you shall not.
Frank Thorney.   Why? Your reason?
Susan. Like to the lapwing have you all this while
   With your false love deluded me, pretending
   Counterfeit senses for your discontent,   155
   And now at last it is by chance stole from you.
Frank Thorney. What! What by chance?
Susan.   Your pre-appointed meeting
   Of single combat with young Warbeck.
Frank Thorney.   Ha!
Susan. Even so! Dissemble not, 'tis too apparent.
   Then in his look I read it. Deny it not,   160
   I see't apparent. Cost it my undoing,
   And unto that my life, I will not leave you.
Frank Thorney. Not until when?
Susan.   Till he and you be friends.
   Was this your cunning, and then flam me off
   With an old witch, two wives and Winnifride?   165
   You're not so kind indeed as I imagined.
Frank Thorney. And you more fond by far than I expected.
   It is a virtue that attends thy kind.
   But of our business within; and by this kiss

---

153. *the lapwing*] Proverbially deceptive in distracting enemies away from
its nest, 'The lapwing cries when furthest from her nest'.
   164. *flam*] deceive by a sham story or trick.
   165. *an old witch*] i.e. the fortune-teller mentioned at ll. 118–19. A wise
woman or white witch as opposed to a black witch such as Elizabeth Sawyer.
   167–8.] Some editors give these lines as an aside, but there is no need for
this, since at one level the lines are complimentary if we take 'fond' as 'loving'
and so can be accepted by Susan. The ironic second sense of 'fond', i.e.
foolish, should be appreciated by the audience.

I'll anger thee no more, troth, chuck, I will not.   170

[*He kisses her.*]

Susan. You shall have no just cause.

Frank Thorney.   Dear Sue, I shall not.

Exeunt.

Act 3

Enter [YOUNG] CUDDY BANKS *and* Morris Dancers.

First Dancer. Nay, Cuddy, prithee do not leave us now. If we part all this night, we shall not meet before day.

Second Dancer. I prithee, Banks, let's keep together now.

Young Banks. If you were wise, a word would serve; but as you are, I must be forced to tell you again I have a little   5
private business, an hour's work; it may prove but an half hour's, as luck may serve, and then I take horse and along with you. Have we e'er a witch in the morris?

First Dancer. No, no; no woman's part but Maid Marian and the hobby-horse.   10

Young Banks. I'll have a witch. I love a witch.

First Dancer. Faith, witches themselves are so common nowadays that the counterfeit will not be regarded. They say we have three or four in Edmonton besides Mother Sawyer.   15

Second Dancer. I would she would dance her part with us.

Third Dancer. So would not I, for, if she comes, the devil and all comes along with her.

Young Banks. Well, I'll have a witch. I have loved a witch ever since I played at cherry-pit. Leave me and get my horse   20
dressed. Give him oats, but water him not till I come. Whither do we foot it first?

---

4. SP. Young Banks] The fact that 1658 text's speech prefix is 'Clown' and continues so for the rest of the play indicates the nature of his role.

If . . . serve] an allusion to the proverb 'A word to a wise man is enough'.

9. *Maid Marian*] the fool's companion in morris dances and May games and latterly associated with Robin Hood; also a cant term for a wanton or a whore.

20. *cherry-pit*] a children's game involving throwing stones into a small pit or hole. Banks's comments have bawdy implications.

22. *foot*] walk, dance.

Second Dancer. To Sir Arthur Clarington's first, then whither
    thou wilt.

Young Banks. Well, I am content. But we must up to Cart-   25
    er's, the rich yeoman. I must be seen on hobby-horse
    there.

First Dancer. Oh, I smell him now. I'll lay my ears Banks is in
    love and that's the reason he would walk melancholy by
    himself.   30

Young Banks. Ha! Who was that said I was in love?

First Dancer. Not I.

Second Dancer. Not I.

Young Banks. Go to, no more of that. When I understand
    what you speak, I know what you say. Believe that.   35

First Dancer. Well, 'twas I, I'll not deny it. I meant no hurt
    in't. I have seen you walk up to Carter's of Chessum.
    Banks, were not you there last Shrovetide?

Young Banks. Yes, I was ten days together there the last
    Shrovetide.   40

Second Dancer. How could that be when there are but seven
    days in the week?

Young Banks. Prithee peace! I reckon *stila nova* as a traveller.
    Thou understandest as a fresh-water farmer that never
    sawest a week beyond sea. Ask any soldier that ever   45

---

28. *smell him*] understand what he's up to.

lay] wager.

34. *Go to*] an expression of disapprobation or incredulity, i.e. 'Come off
it!'.

37. *Chessum*] Cheshunt in Hertfordshire, some four miles north of
Edmonton.

38. *Shrovetide*] the week before the beginning of Lent (the period of
fasting before Easter), which was given over to festivity. Shrovetide lingers on
as Shrove Tuesday when it is traditional to prepare and eat pancakes.

43. stila nova . . . *traveller*] literally, 'of the new style as a traveller'. Young
Banks jokingly refers to the revised calendar introduced by Pope Gregory
in 1582 which corrected the accumulated errors of the Julian calendar
established by Julius Caesar. Because of its Roman Catholic associations
the Gregorian calendar was not adopted in England until 1752 when the
date had to be advanced by ten days to achieve parity with continental
practice.

44. *fresh-water farmer*] landlubber.

45–7. *Ask . . . there*] a reference to the unpunctuality of soldiers' pay.

received his pay but in the Low Countries, and he'll tell
thee there are eight days in the week there hard by. How
dost thou think they rise in High Germany, Italy and
those remoter places?

Third Dancer. Ay, but simply there are but seven days in the   50
week yet.

Young Banks. No, simply as thou understandest. Prithee,
look but in the lover's almanac. When he has been but
three days absent, 'Oh', says he, 'I have not seen my love
these seven years. There's a long cut.' When he comes   55
to her again, and embraces her, 'Oh', says he, 'now
methinks I am in heaven', and that's a pretty step. He
that can get up to heaven in ten days need not repent his
journey. You may ride a hundred days in a caroche, and
be further off than when you set forth. But, I pray you,   60
good morris mates, now leave me. I will be with you by
midnight.

First Dancer. Well, since he will be alone, we'll back again and
trouble him no more.

All. But remember, Banks.   65

Young Banks. The hobby-horse shall be remembered. But
hark you, get Poldavis, the barber's boy, for the witch,
because he can show his art better than another.

                    Exeunt [all but YOUNG BANKS].

Well, now to my walk. I am near the place where I should
meet I know not what. Say I meet a thief, I must follow   70
him, if to the gallows. Say I meet a horse, or hare, or

---

46. *Low Countries*] the modern Netherlands and Belgium, also a
euphemism for female genitalia. See Shakespeare's *The Comedy of Errors*,
3.2.141–3.

47. *hard by*] very nearly.

48. *rise*] get up in the morning, regulate their time. Banks blinds his
companion with science.

55. *cut*] misfortune, but with bawdy implications.

59. *caroche*] coach.

66. *The hobby-horse . . . remembered*] Banks reverses the common saying
'The Hobby-horse shall be forgot' (see *Hamlet*, 3.2.120) which seems to have
been the refrain of a contemporary ballad referring to the energetic recovery
of the horse after apparent death in May Day games as seen in the Padstow
May Day celebrations to this day.

67. *Poldavis*] See note 15 on Actors' Names.

hound, still I must follow. Some slow-paced beast, I
hope; yet love is full of lightness in the heaviest lovers.

[Enter DOG.]

Ha! My guide is come. A water-dog. I am thy first man,
Sculler. I go with thee. Ply no other but myself. Away   75
with the boat. Land me but at Katherine's Dock, my
sweet Katherine's Dock, and I'll be a fare to thee. [*Dog
leads.*] That way? Nay, which way thou wilt, thou knowst
the way better than I. [*Aside*] Fine gentle cur it is, and
well brought up, I warrant him. [*To Dog*] We go a-   80
ducking, spaniel; thou shalt fetch me the ducks, pretty
kind rascal.

Enter [*a*] SPIRIT *in shape of* KATHERINE,
vizarded, and takes it off.

Spirit. [*Aside*] Thus throw I off mine own essential horror,
  And take the shape of a sweet lovely maid
  Whom this fool dotes on. We can meet his folly,   85
  But from his virtues must be runaways.

---

73. *heaviest*] most serious, but also referring to his weight.

74. *water-dog*] a dog trained to retrieve waterfowl during hunting. The
term allows Young Banks to indulge in a series of extended water puns and
references.

I am . . . man] the common cry of the watermen plying for hire on the
River Thames.

76. *Katherine's Dock*] Young Banks puns on his love's name and the
Thames landing place near Saint Katherine's Hospital east of the Tower of
London. 'Dock' also suggests bawdy play.

80–1. *a-ducking*] hunting wild duck.

82.1–2.] It is likely that the boy actor playing Katherine would also play
the Spirit who enters 'vizarded' (i.e. in a devil's mask) which he then removes
to appear as Katherine.

84.] The way in which spirits achieved physical manifestation was a matter
of some debate. Theologically the devil was unable to create a body for a
spirit to inhabit, since the creative act was held to be God's prerogative. In
Jonson's *The Devil is an Ass* (1.1.135–6) Satan tells the minor devil that in
order to ascend to Earth he must 'Take a body ready-made . . . I can create
you none'.

85–6. *We . . . runaways*] The Spirit acknowledges that whilst it can exploit
Banks's foolishness, his basic virtues protect him from serious harm. See
2.1.164n.

We'll sport with him, but when we reckoning call,
We know where to receive. Th' witch pays for all.

Dog barks.

Young Banks. Ay? Is that the watchword? She's come. Well, if
ever we be married, it shall be at Barking Church in   90
memory of thee. Now come behind, kind cur.

And have I met thee, sweet Kate?
I will teach thee to walk so late.

Oh, see, we meet in metre. What? Dost thou trip from
me? Oh, that I were upon my hobby-horse! I would   95
mount after thee so nimble.

'Stay, nymph, stay, nymph,' singed Apollo.
Tarry and kiss me, sweet nymph, stay.
Tarry and kiss me, sweet.
We will to Chessum Street,   100
And then to the house stands in the highway.

Nay, by your leave, I must embrace you.

[*Exeunt* SPIRIT *and* YOUNG BANKS.]

[*Within*] Oh, help, help! I am drowned, I am drowned!
Dog. Ha, ha, ha, ha!

Enter [YOUNG BANKS] *wet.*

Young Banks. This was an ill night to go a-wooing in; I find it   105
now in Pond's Almanac. Thinking to land at Katherine's
Dock, I was almost at Gravesend. I'll never go to a wench

---

88. *receive*] claim our due.

90. *Barking Church*] All Hallows, Barking, on the north side of Great
Tower Street. Close to the Tower of London, it is now generally known as
All Hallows-by-the-Tower.

97–101.] Young Banks adapts a popular ballad, 'When Daphne Did from
Phoebus Fly', to his own purposes, since lovers traditionally fell into verse:
When Daphne from fair Phoebus did fly,
The west wind did most sweetly blow in her face:
Her silken scarf scarce shadowed her eyes;
The god cried 'O pity,' and held her in chase.
'Stay, nymph, stay, nymph,' cries Apollo,
'Tarry and turn thee; sweet nymph, stay!'

106. *Pond's Almanac*] a popular almanac annually published in London
from 1604 by Edward Pond. Young Banks's speeches contain a number of
such laboured puns.

107. *Gravesend*] a port in Kent on the south bank of the Thames, thirty
miles below London, whose name lends itself to obvious wordplay.

in the dog-days again. Yet 'tis cool enough. Had you
never a paw in this dog-trick? A mangie take that black
hide of yours! I'll throw you in at Limehouse in some   110
tanner's pit or other.

Dog. Ha, ha, ha, ha!

Young Banks. How now! Who's that laughs at me? Hist to
him.   *Dog barks.*

Peace, peace! Thou didst but thy kind neither. 'Twas my   115
own fault.

Dog. Take heed how thou trustest the devil another time.

Young Banks. How now! Who's that speaks? I hope you have
not your reading tongue about you?

Dog. Yes, I can speak.   120

Young Banks. The devil you can! You have read Aesop's
fables, then. I have played one of your parts there, the dog
that catched at the shadow in the water. Pray you, let me
catechise you a little. What might one call your name,
dog?   125

Dog. My dame calls me Tom.

Young Banks. 'Tis well, and she may call me Ass, so there's an
whole one betwixt us, Tom-Ass. She said I should follow
you, indeed. Well, Tom, give me thy fist, we are friends.
You shall be mine ingle. I love you, but I pray you let's   130
have no more of these ducking devices.

---

108. *dog-days*] the hottest and most unwholesome days of the year between the beginning of July and mid-August. It was widely believed that dogs
were apt to go mad at this season. The sun at this time is near Sirius, the dog
star.

109. *dog-trick*] treacherous or spiteful act.

mangie] mange.

110. *Limehouse*] a district, noted for its tanneries, on the north bank of the
Thames opposite Cuckold's Haven.

113. *Hist*] listen.

115. *Thou . . . neither*] i.e. 'You only did what came naturally to you'.

118–19. *I hope . . . you*] Young Banks fears that the Dog is about to read
him a sermon.

121–3. *Aesop's . . . water*] Aesop tells of a dog who, carrying a stolen piece
of meat in his mouth whilst crossing a bridge, and seeing his reflection in the
water below, lost his prize in attempting to rob his supposed rival.

122. *there*] Gifford's emendation makes better sense than quarto's 'then',
which appears to be a compositor's eye-slip from the previous 'then'.

124. *catechise*] question, interrogate.

126.] as in Goodcole. See Appendix, p. 144.

130. *ingle*] strictly a boy-favourite, but here a familiar friend or chum.

Dog. Not, if you love me. Dogs love where they are beloved.
    Cherish me, and I'll do anything for thee.
Young Banks. Well, you shall have jowls and livers. I have
    butchers to my friends that shall bestow 'em, and I will   135
    keep crusts and bones for you, if you'll be a kind dog,
    Tom.
Dog. Anything. I'll help thee to thy love.
Young Banks. Wilt thou? That promise shall cost me a brown
    loaf, though I steal it out of my father's cupboard. You'll   140
    eat stolen goods, Tom, will you not?
Dog. Oh, best of all. The sweetest bits, those.
Young Banks. You shall not starve, Ningle Tom, believe that.
    If you love fish, I'll help you to maids and soles. I'm
    acquainted with a fishmonger.   145
Dog. Maids and soles? Oh, sweet bits! Banqueting stuff,
    those.
Young Banks. One thing I would request you, Ningle, as you
    have played the knavish cur with me a little, that you
    would mingle amongst our morris dancers in the morn-   150
    ing. You can dance?
Dog. Yes, yes, anything. I'll be there, but unseen to any but
    thyself. Get thee gone before. Fear not my presence. I
    have work tonight. I serve more masters, more dames,
    than one.   155
Young Banks. [*Aside*] He can serve mammon and the devil
    too!
Dog. It shall concern thee and thy love's purchase.
    There's a gallant rival loves the maid,

---

134. *jowls*] jaw-bones.

135. *to*] among.

143. *Ningle*] i.e. mine ingle. See note to 130 above.

144–5. *If you . . . fishmonger*] another example of Young Banks's extended
word-play with bawdy implications. At the level of fish, 'maids' are young
skate or thornback whilst 'soles' are flatfish. However, 'fishmonger' is a cant
term for a pimp or procurer, which suggests a darker meaning, i.e. Banks can
supply Dog not only with virgin prostitutes but also with souls.

154–7. *I . . . too*] Both characters allude to Biblical sayings, Luke, 16.13
and Matt., 6.24, 'No servant can serve two masters' and 'Ye cannot serve
God and Mammon'. Such precepts became proverbial.

159. *gallant rival*] Somerton.

And likely is to have her. Mark what a mischief,   160
    Before the morris ends, shall light on him.
Young Banks. Oh, sweet Ningle, thy neuf once again. Friends
    must part for a time. Farewell, with this remembrance:
    shalt have bread too when we meet again. If ever there
    were an honest devil, 'twill be the Devil of Edmonton, I   165
    see. Farewell, Tom. I prithee, dog me as soon as thou
    canst.   *Exit* [YOUNG] BANKS.
Dog. I'll not miss thee, and be merry with thee.
    Those that are joys denied must take delight
    In sins and mischiefs; 'tis the devil's right.   *Exit* DOG.   170

3.2

Enter YOUNG [FRANK] THORNEY, WINNIFRIDE
as a boy [*weeping*].

Frank Thorney. Prithee no more. Those tears give
        nourishment
    To weeds and briers in me, which shortly will
    O'ergrow and top my head. My shame will sit
    And cover all that can be seen of me.
Winnifride. I have not shown this cheek in company;   5
    Pardon me now. Thus singled with yourself,
    It calls a thousand sorrows round about;
    Some going before and some on either side,

160–1. *Mark . . . him*] The Dog's words suggest that not only does he
prompt Frank's murder of Susan but that he also prompts the blaming of the
murder on Somerton and Warbeck.

161. *light*] alight, befall.

162. *neuf*] fist.

162–3. *Friends . . . time*] Proverbial: 'Farewell and be hanged, friends
must part'.

165. *Devil of Edmonton*] an allusion to Peter Fabell, the hero of *The Merry
Devil of Edmonton* (1602) who helped a couple to marry in the face of parental
opposition.

166. *dog*] follow (with obvious pun).

3. *top*] cover.

5. *cheek*] i.e. tearful cheek.

6. *singled*] alone.

7. *It calls*] i.e. my tearful cheek recalls.

But infinite behind; all chained together.
Your second, adulterous marriage leads,   10
That's the sad eclipse: the effects must follow
As plagues of shame, spite, scorn and obloquy.
Frank Thorney. Why? Hast thou not left one hour's patience
To add to all the rest? One hour bears us
Beyond the reach of all these enemies.   15
Are we not now set forward in the flight,
Provided with the dowry of my sin
To keep us in some other nation?
While we together are, we are at home
In any place.
Winnifride.   'Tis foul ill-gotten coin,   20
Far worse than usury or extortion.
Frank Thorney. Let my father then make the restitution,
Who forced me take the bribe. It is his gift
And patrimony to me; so I receive it.
He would not bless, nor look a father on me,   25
Until I satisfied his angry will.
When I was sold, I sold myself again—
Some knaves have done't in lands, and I in body—
For money, and I have the hire. But, sweet, no more;
'Tis hazard of discovery, our discourse,   30
And then prevention takes off all our hopes.
For only but to take her leave of me
My wife is coming.
Winnifride.   Who coming? Your wife!
Frank Thorney. No, no, thou art here. The woman, I knew

10.] It is apparent from the manner of Winnifride's entry that she has recently learnt of Frank's marriage to Susan. By the avoidance of a scene which presents this discovery, the dramatists focus attention on the *consequences* of the action. In performance the audience will attribute their own knowledge of the action to Winnifride. Such economy is a mark of mature dramatic writing.

11. *eclipse*] An eclipse was often regarded as a portent of future misfortune.

17. *the dowry . . . sin*] i.e. the moneys which Frank acquired by his marriage to Susan.

29. *hire*] payment, wages.

30–1.] i.e. 'our continuing conversation invites discovery of our secret relationship, and thus all our hopes and plans could be destroyed'.

34. *here*] Dyce's conjectural reading 'her' is possible, but emendation is unnecessary since the quarto reading makes good sense.

Not how to call her now, but after this day   35
She shall be quite forgot and have no name
In my remembrance. See, see, she's come.

Enter SUSAN.

Go lead
The horses to the hill's top; there I'll meet thee.
Susan. Nay, with your favour, let him stay a little.
I would part with him too, because he is   40
Your sole companion, and I'll begin with him,
Reserving you the last.
Frank Thorney.   Ay, with all my heart.
Susan. You may hear, if it please you, sir.
Frank Thorney.   No, 'tis not fit.
Some rudiments, I conceive, they must be,
To overlook my slippery footings. And so—   45
Susan. No, indeed, sir.
Frank Thorney.   Tush, I know it must be so
And 'tis necessary. On, but be brief.   [*He walks aside.*]
Winnifride. What charge soe'er you lay upon me, mistress,
I shall support it faithfully, being honest,
To my best strength.   50
Susan. Believe't shall be no other. I know you were
Commended to my husband by a noble knight.
Winnifride. Oh, gods! Oh, mine eyes!
Susan.   How now? What ailst thou, lad?
Winnifride. Something hit mine eye; it makes it water still,
Even as you said 'commended to my husband'.   55
Some dor I think it was. I was, forsooth.
Commended to him by Sir Arthur Clarington.
Susan. Whose servant once my Thorney was himself.
That title, methinks, should make you almost fellows,
Or at the least much more than a servant,   60
And I am sure he will respect you so.

---

39. *him*] Susan thinks Winnifride a boy because of her disguise.

44. *rudiments*] elementary instructions.

45. *overlook . . . footings*] i.e. 'make sure I don't slip or fall'. Frank's phrasing will have a darker meaning for the audience who know of his previous transgressions.

48. *charge*] duty.

56. *dor*] fly or flying insect.

Your love to him, then, needs no spur from me,
And what for my sake you will ever do,
'Tis fit it should be bought with something more
Than fair entreats. Look, here's a jewel for thee,   65
                              [*Giving a jewel*]
A pretty wanton label for thine ear,
And I would have it hang there, still to whisper
These words to thee: 'Thou hast my jewel with thee'.
It is but earnest of a larger bounty
When thou returnest with praises of thy service,   70
Which I am confident thou wilt deserve.
Why, thou art many now besides thyself.
Thou mayst be servant, friend and wife to him.
A good wife is them all. A friend can play
The wife and servant's part, and shift enough,   75
No less the servant can the friend and wife.
'Tis all but sweet society, good counsel,
Interchanged loves, yes, and counsel-keeping.
Frank Thorney. Not done yet?
Susan. Even now, sir.   80
Winnifride. Mistress, believe my vow. Your severe eye,
Were it present to command, your bounteous hand,
Were it then by to buy or bribe my service,
Shall not make me more dear or near unto him
Than I shall voluntary. I'll be all your charge: 85
Servant, friend, wife to him.
Susan.   Wilt thou?
Now blessings go with thee for't! Courtesies
Shall meet thee coming home.
Winnifride.   Pray you, say plainly,
Mistress, are you jealous of him? If you be,
I'll look to him that way too.
Susan.   Sayst thou so?   90

---

66. *label*] literally a strip of material used to attach a seal to a document or
a tassel, but here, since Susan gives Winnifride a jewel, a pendant earring.
68. *my jewel*] also meaning her chastity.
69. *earnest . . . bounty*] first instalment of a substantial reward.
75. *shift enough*] perform the role well enough.
89. *jealous*] mistrustful.
90. *look to*] keep watch on.

I would thou hadst a woman's bosom now.
We have weak thoughts within us. Alas,
There's nothing so strong in us as suspicion.
But I dare not, nay, I will not think
So hardly of my Thorney.
Winnifride.   Believe it, mistress,   95
    I'll be no pander to him, and if I find
    Any loose lubric scapes in him, I'll watch him,
    And at my return protest I'll show you all.
    He shall hardly offend without my knowledge.
Susan. Thine own diligence is that I press,   100
    And not the curious eye over his faults.
    Farewell. If I should never see thee more,
    Take it for ever.
Frank Thorney. Prithee take that along with thee,
                [*He*] *gives his sword* [*to Winnifride*].
                        and haste thee
    To the hill's top. I'll be there instantly.   105
Susan. No haste, I prithee; slowly as thou canst.
                        Exit WINNIFRIDE.
    Pray let him obey me now; 'tis happily
    His last service to me. My power is e'en
    A-going out of sight.
Frank Thorney.   Why would you delay?
    We have no other business now but to part.   110
Susan. And will not that, sweetheart, ask a long time?
    Methinks it is the hardest piece of work
    That e'er I took in hand.
Frank Thorney.   Fie, fie! Why look,
    I'll make it plain and easy to you. Farewell.
                        Kisses [*her*].
Susan. Ah, 'las! I am not half perfect in it yet.   115
    I must have it read over an hundred times.

---

97. *lubric*] lascivious, wanton.
scapes] infidelities, transgressions.
98. *protest*] vow.
100. *that I press*] what I urge.
103. *it*] i.e. the label.
107. *happily*] perhaps.
111. *ask*] take.

Pray you take some pains; I confess my dullness.

Frank Thorney. [*Aside*] What a thorn this rose grows on!
    Parting were sweet,
    But what a trouble 'twill be to obtain it!
    [*To her*] Come.   *Kisses* [*her*].
                    Again and again. Farewell. Yet wilt return?   120
    All questions of my journey, my stay, employment
    And revisitation, fully I have answered all.
    There's nothing now behind, but nothing.

Susan. And that nothing is more hard than anything,
    Than all the everythings. This request—

Frank Thorney.   What is it?   125

Susan. That I may bring you through one pasture more
    Up to yon knot of trees. Amongst those shadows
    I'll vanish from you; they shall teach me how.

Frank Thorney. Why, 'tis granted. Come, walk then.

Susan.   Nay, not too fast.
    They say slow things have best perfection;   130
    The gentle shower wets to fertility,
    The churlish storm may mischief with his bounty;
    The baser beasts take strength, even from the womb,
    But the lord lion's whelp is feeble long.   *Exeunt.*

3.3

Enter DOG.

Dog. Now for an early mischief and a sudden.
    The mind's about it now. One touch from me
    Soon sets the body forward.

---

123. *behind*] hidden, secret.
130.] a variation of the proverb 'Slow but sure'.
132. *mischief*] do harm.
133–4.] Examples of such views are to be found in Pliny, *Natural History*,
8.15 (trans. P. Holland, 1601), p. 201, and Edward Topsell, *The History of
Four-footed Beasts* (1607), p. 466.

0.1.] The Dog is invisible in this scene to all but the audience.
2. *The . . . now*] i.e. 'The mind is already scheming'. The text is ambiguous in that the Dog may be referring to its own plotting or perhaps to Frank's
subconscious impulses.

Enter YOUNG [FRANK] THORNEY [*and*] SUSAN.

Frank Thorney. Your request is out. Yet will you leave me?
Susan.   What?
     So churlishly? You'll make me stay for ever,   5
     Rather than part with such a sound from you.
Frank Thorney. Why, you almost anger me. Pray you, be
          gone.
     You have no company, and 'tis very early;
     Some hurt may betide you homewards.
Susan.   Tush! I fear none.
     To leave you is the greatest hurt I can suffer.   10
     Besides, I expect your father and mine own
     To meet me back, or overtake me with you.
     They began to stir when I came after you;
     I know they'll not be long.
Frank Thorney. [*Aside*]   So, I shall have more trouble.
                                      Dog rubs him.
     Thank you for that. Then I'll ease all at once.   15
     'Tis done now, what I ne'er thought on.
                         [*To her*] You shall not go back.
Susan. Why? Shall I go along with thee? Sweet music!
Frank Thorney. No, to a better place.
Susan.   Any place, I.
     I'm there at home where thou pleasest to have me.

---

4. *Your . . . out*] i.e. 'We have come as far as you asked'.

9. *betide*] befall.

12. *back*] on the way back.

14.1.] The degree to which the Dog's action provokes Susan's murder is
unclear. It has been suggested that by means of the Dog's touch Frank is
possessed by the devil. Alternatively, in view of Dog's remarks at 2.1.164–6
and ll. 2–3 above, the action serves to prompt Frank's hidden or unconscious
impulses. See also 4.1.203.1n.

15. *Thank . . . that*] Frank here appears to be subconsciously responding
to the Dog's action in rubbing against him rather than speaking directly to
Susan. Thus it seems preferable to take the whole of his speech as an aside
articulating the inner stirrings of his murderous intent. Whilst, superficially,
it is possible to interpret Frank's lines as an expression of his gratitude to
Susan for her reminder that Old Carter and Old Thorney are expected, the
audience cannot but apply Frank's thanks to the Dog.

18. *a better place*] i.e. heaven, though Susan understands this to mean 'at
home'.

Frank Thorney. At home? I'll leave you in your last lodging.   20
    I must kill you.

Susan.   Oh, fine! You'd fright me from you.

Frank Thorney. You see I had no purpose. I'm unarmed.
    'Tis this minute's decree, and it must be.
    Look, this will serve your turn.   [*He takes a knife.*]

Susan.   I'll not turn from it
    If you be earnest, sir. Yet you may tell me   25
    Wherefore you'll kill me.

Frank Thorney.   Because you are a whore.

Susan. There's one deep wound already—a whore?
    'Twas ever further from me than the thought
    Of this black hour. A whore?

Frank Thorney.   Yes, I'll prove it,
    And you shall confess it. You are my whore.   30
    No wife of mine. The word admits no second.
    I was before wedded to another, have her still.
    I do not lay the sin unto your charge;
    'Tis all mine own. Your marriage was my theft,
    For I espoused your dowry, and I have it.   35
    I did not purpose to have added murder;
    The devil did not prompt me. Till this minute
    You might have safe returned; now you cannot.
    You have dogged your own death.   *Stabs her.*

Susan.   And I deserve it.
    I'm glad my fate was so intelligent.   40

---

20. *your last lodging*] your grave.

21. *Oh, fine!*] i.e. 'Oh, how skilful!'

23. *'Tis . . . decree*] i.e. 'The idea has only just occurred to me'. The dramatists stress Frank's unpreparedness; note that he has previously given his sword to Winnifride at 3.2.104.

24. *Look . . . turn*] The quarto text gives no clue as to where the knife comes from. Since he has given up his sword and states that he is unarmed (l. 22), it seems most likely that the Dog provides the knife. Line 24's 'Look, this will serve your turn' suggests Frank's surprise at finding a weapon. Such an interpretation is supported by his failure to recognise the Dog's assistance at l. 71.1 where he helps Frank to tie himself up as a means of securing an alibi.

39. *dogged*] pursued or tracked like a dog (with obvious irony).

40. *intelligent*] intelligible, understandable.

'Twas some good spirit's motion. Die? Oh, 'twas time!
How many years might I have slept in sin?
Sin of my most hatred too, adultery!

Frank Thorney. Nay, sure, 'twas likely that the most was past,
For I meant never to return to you   45
After this parting.

Susan.   Why, then I thank you more.
You have done lovingly, leaving yourself,
That you would thus bestow me on another.
Thou art my husband, Death, and I embrace thee
With all the love I have. Forget the stain   50
Of my unwitting sin, and then I come
A crystal virgin to thee. My soul's purity
Shall with bold wings ascend the doors of Mercy,
For Innocence is ever her companion.

Frank Thorney. Not yet mortal? I would not linger you,   55
Or leave you a tongue to blab.   [*He stabs her again.*]

Susan. Now heaven reward you ne'er the worse for me!
I did not think that Death had been so sweet,
Nor I so apt to love him. I could ne'er die better,
Had I stayed forty years for preparation,   60
For I'm in charity with all the world.
Let me for once be thine example, heaven.
Do to this man as I him free forgive,
And may he better die and better live.   *She dies.*

Frank Thorney. 'Tis done, and I am in! Once past our height,   65
We scorn the deep'st abyss. This follows now,

---

41. *'Twas ... motion*] Susan's comment is sharply ironic, since the audience recognises that the devil has had a hand in crystallising Frank's murderous intention. Although Roman Catholics held that there were personal good spirits or guardian angels, such beliefs were held to be superstitious by most Protestant theologians and writers. See Keith Thomas, *Religion and the Decline of Magic*, 1971 (repr. 1978), pp. 562 and 589.

44. *most*] worst.

55. *mortal*] dead.

linger] delay.

61. *in charity*] at peace, in a state of Christian reconciliation.

65. *I am in*] i.e. 'I am completely lost'; cf. *Macbeth*, 3.4.137–8, 'I am in blood / Stepped in so far . . .'

To heal her wounds by dressing of the weapon:
Arms, thighs, hands, any place, we must not fail
                              Wounds himself.
Light scratches, giving such deep ones. The best I can
To bind myself to this tree. Now's the storm,   70
Which, if blown o'er, many fair days may follow.
                              Dog ties him.
So, so, I'm fast. I did not think I could
Have done so well behind me. How prosperous
And effectual mischief sometimes is.——Help! Help!
Murder, murder, murder!   *Exit* DOG.   75

          Enter [OLD] CARTER *and* OLD THORNEY.

Old Carter. Ha! Whom tolls the bell for?
Frank Thorney.   Oh! Oh!
Old Thorney.   Ah me!
    The cause appears too soon; my child, my son!
Old Carter. Susan, girl, child! Not speak to thy father? Ha!
Frank Thorney. Oh, lend me some assistance to o'ertake
    This hapless woman!
Old Thorney.   Let's o'ertake the murderers.   80
    Speak whilst thou canst, anon may be too late.
    I fear thou hast death's mark upon thee too.
Frank Thorney. I know them both, yet such an oath is passed
    As pulls damnation up if it be broke.
    I dare not name 'em. Think what forced men do.   85

---

67. *heal*] i.e. 'conceal the source of'.
    dressing . . . weapon] i.e. 'directing or managing the weapon in order to wound myself and thus allay any suspicion of my guilt', with an ironic play on 'dressing' in the sense of 'tending a wound'.
    68. *fail*] flinch from.
    75. SD] It is possible for the Dog to exit having retrieved the knife for subsequent use (see 4.2.68n).
    76. *Whom tolls the bell for*] a familiar saying, alluding to the tolling of the church bell for a death. Old Carter presumably responds to Frank's cry, though it seems unlikely that he realises at this stage that a death has occurred.
    79. *o'ertake*] i.e. in death.
    80. *hapless*] unlucky, unfortunate.
    84.] i.e. 'as will pull damnation upon me if the oath were to be broken'.
    85. *Think . . . do*] i.e. 'Consider what men subjected to violence may be forced to do'.

Old Thorney. Keep oath with murderers? That were a
    conscience
    To hold the devil in.
Frank Thorney.   Nay, sir, I can describe 'em;
    Shall show them as familiar as their names.
    The taller of the two at this time wears
    His satin doublet white but crimson lined,   90
    Hose of black satin, cloak of scarlet—
Old Thorney. Warbeck, Warbeck, Warbeck!
                [*To Old Carter*] Do you list to this, sir?
Old Carter. Yes, yes, I listen you. Here's nothing to be heard.
Frank Thorney. Th'other's cloak branched velvet, black,
    velvet-lined
    His suit.
Old Thorney. I have 'em already; Somerton, Somerton!   95
    Binal revenge all this. Come, sir, the first work
    Is to pursue the murderers, when we have removed
    These mangled bodies hence.
Old Carter. Sir, take that carcass there, and give me this.
    I'll not own her now, she's none of mine.   100
    Bob me off with a dumb-show? No, I'll have life.
    This is my son too, and while there's life in him,
    'Tis half mine. Take you half that silence for't.
    When I speak I look to be spoken to.
    Forgetful slut!
Old Thorney.   Alas, what grief may do now!   105
    Look, sir, I'll take this load of sorrow with me.
Old Carter. Ay, do, and I'll have this.—How do you, sir?
Frank Thorney. Oh, very ill, sir.

---

93. *listen*] listen to.

Here's . . . heard] Old Carter refers to Susan.

94. *branched*] embroidered with a figured pattern representing flowers or
foliage.

96. *Binal*] double, twofold.

99. *this*] i.e. Frank (seemingly dying). See also l. 107.

100. *own*] acknowledge.

101. *Bob me off*] fool me, mock me.

dumb-show] silent display; here Susan's lifeless body.

103. *Take . . . for't*] i.e. 'Take half of the dead and silent Susan'.

106. *load of sorrow*] Old Thorney carries Susan's body.

107. *I'll have this*] Old Carter assists Frank to rise.

Old Carter. Yes, I think so, but 'tis well you can speak yet.
 There's no music but in sound, sound it must be. 110
 I have not wept these twenty years before,
 And that I guess was ere that girl was born.
 Yet now methinks, if I but knew the way,
 My heart's so full, I could weep night and day.
       Exeunt [with Susan's body].

3·4

    Enter SIR ARTHUR CLARINGTON, WARBECK
      [*and*] SOMERTON.

Sir Arthur. Come, gentlemen, we must all help to grace
 The nimble-footed youth of Edmonton,
 That are so kind to call us up today
 With an high morris.
Warbeck. I could wish it for the best it were the worst now. Ab- 5
 surdity's in my opinion ever the best dancer in a morris.
Somerton. I could rather sleep than see 'em.
Sir Arthur. Not well, sir?
Somerton. 'Faith, not ever thus leaden, yet I know no cause
 for't. 10
Warbeck. Now am I beyond mine own condition highly dis-
 posed to mirth.
Sir Arthur. Well, you may have yet a morris to help both;
 To strike you in a dump, and make him merry.

    Enter [SAWGUT *the*] *fiddler and* [*the*] *morris; all but*
      [YOUNG] BANKS.

Sawgut. Come, will you set yourselves in morris ray? The 15
 fore-bell, second-bell, tenor and great-bell; Maid Marian

---

4. *high*] high-class or, perhaps, high-spirited.
5.] i.e. 'I hope that this is the worst we have to put up with'.
9. *leaden*] in low spirits, depressed.
14. *dump*] black mood.
him] Somerton.
15. *morris ray*] morris array, position or formation for the dance.
15–17. *The . . . bell*] Despite Cuddy's declaration that he would have all
trebles, no *means*, or *basses*, Sawgut's arrangement includes counters, tenors

for the same bell. But where's the weather-cock now?
The hobby-horse?
First Dancer. Is not Banks come yet? What a spite 'tis!
Sir Arthur. When set you forward, gentlemen?   20
Second Dancer. We stay but for the hobby-horse, sir. All our
        footmen are ready.
Somerton. 'Tis marvel your horse should be behind your foot.
Second Dancer. Yes, sir, he goes further about. We can come
        in at the wicket, but the broad gate must be opened for   25
        him.

>   *Enter* [YOUNG] BANKS, [*as*] Hobby-Horse, *and* DOG.

Sir Arthur. Oh, we stayed for you, sir.
Young Banks. Only my horse wanted a shoe, sir, but we shall
        make you amends ere we part.
Sir Arthur. Ay? Well said. Make 'em drink ere they begin.   30

>   *Enter* Servants *with beer.*

Young Banks. A bowl, I prithee, and a little for my horse;
        he'll mount the better. Nay, give me. I must drink to him,
        he'll not pledge else. [*He drinks.*] Here, Hobby.
>   *Holds him the bowl.*
I pray you. No? Not drink? You see, gentlemen, we can

---

and basses as usual. The dramatists should not be criticised for inconsistency
since their chief interest in 2.1. lies in exploiting the comic possibilities of
Cuddy's punning.

17. *weather-cock*] weather-vane in the shape of a cock, often placed at the
top of a church spire, here suggesting both the instability of the hobby-horse
(made of light wood) and also Cuddy's changeability and fickleness.

19. *spite*] i.e. bother, nuisance.

22. *footmen*] dancers.

23. *should . . . foot*] i.e. 'should be delayed, given that cavalry move more
quickly than infantry'. Or this may be a joke about a horse usually going in
front of the men (in ploughing or riding a cart).

24. *goes further about*] takes the long way round.

25. *wicket*] small gate for pedestrians.

26.1. and DOG] The Dog is understood to be invisible to all but Cuddy
and the audience.

32. *mount*] perform, with bawdy implications.

33. *pledge*] drink a health.

34–6. *we . . . no*] Proverbial, 'A man can lead a horse to the water but he
cannot make him drink unless he will'.

but bring our horse to the water; he may choose whether   35
he'll drink or no.

Somerton. A good moral made plain by history.

Second Dancer. Strike up, Father Sawgut, strike up.

Sawgut. E'en when you will, children. Now in the name of the
best foot forward. How now! Not a word in thy guts? I   40
think, children, my instrument has caught cold on the
sudden.

Young Banks. [*Aside*] My ningle's knavery; Black Tom's
doing.

All. Why, what mean you, Father Sawgut?   45

Young Banks. Why, what would you have him do? You hear
his fiddle is speechless.

Sawgut. I'll lay mine ear to my instrument that my poor fiddle
is bewitched. I played 'The Flowers in May' e'en now
as sweet as a violet. Now 'twill not go against the hair.   50
You see, I can make no more music than a beetle of a
cow-turd.

Young Banks. Let me see, Father Sawgut. Say once you had
a brave hobby-horse that you were beholding to. I'll play
and dance too. [*Aside*] Ningle, away with it.   55

All. Ay, marry, sir.

> *Dog plays the morris;* [*the Dancers give their morris;*] *which*
> *ended, enter a* Constable *and* Officers.

Constable. Away with jollity! 'Tis too sad an hour.

---

40. *Not . . . guts?*] Not a sound from your belly? (Fiddle strings were
usually made of cat gut.)

48–9. *my poor . . . bewitched*] Cf. Heywood and Brome's *The Late Lancashire Witches* (1634), 3.1. where the fiddlers are also bewitched.

49. *The Flowers in May*] a dance tune now lost.

50. *against the hair*] against the grain.

51–2. *I . . . cow-turd*] Proverbial, a version of 'The beetle flies over many
a sweet flower and lights in a cowshard'.

54. *brave*] excellent.

beholding to] indebted to.

56.1. *Dog . . . morris*] Despite the worries of previous editors, audiences
have little difficulty in accepting the dramatic convention of invisibility. The
1981 RSC production made no attempt to signal or hint at the Dog's invisible
status, which the audience easily accepted, even to the point of the Dog
playing the fiddle handed to him by Banks. Cf. the handling of invisibility in
A Midsummer Night's Dream, 3.1.

Sir Arthur Clarington, your own assistance,
In the King's name, I charge, for apprehension
Of these two murderers, Warbeck and Somerton.　　　60
Sir Arthur. Ha! Flat murderers?
Somerton. Ha, ha, ha! This has awakened my melancholy.
Warbeck. And struck my mirth down flat. Murderers?
Constable. The accusation is flat against you, gentlemen.
　　[*To Sir Arthur*] Sir, you may be satisfied with this.　　　65
　　　　　　　　　　　　[*He shows his warrant.*]
I hope you'll quietly obey my power;
'Twill make your cause the fairer.
Somerton and Warbeck. Oh, with all our hearts, sir.
Young Banks. [*Aside*] There's my rival taken up for hang-
　　man's meat. Tom told me he was about a piece of vil-　　　70
　　lainy.—Mates and morris men, you see here's no longer
　　piping, no longer dancing. This news of murder has slain
　　the morris. You that go the footway, fare ye well. I am for
　　a gallop. Come, Ningle.
　　　　　　　　　Exe[*unt* YOUNG BANKS *and* DOG].
Sawgut. (*Strikes his fiddle.*) Ay? Nay, an my fiddle be come to　　　75
　　himself again, I care not. I think the devil has been abroad
　　amongst us today. I'll keep thee out of thy fit now, if I
　　can.
　　　　　　　Exeunt [SAWGUT *and* Morris Dancers].
Sir Arthur. [*To Constable*] These things are full of horror,
　　full of pity.
But if this time be constant to the proof,　　　80
The guilt of both these gentlemen I dare take
Upon mine own danger. Yet, howsoever, sir,
Your power must be obeyed.
Warbeck.　　　　　　　　Oh, most willingly, sir.
'Tis a most sweet affliction! I could not meet
A joy in the best shape with better will.　　　85

---

59. *charge*] order, command.

61. *Flat*] undeniable, downright.

77. *fit*] a sudden and transitory state of inaction (*OED* 4a) or a paroxysm of lunacy.

80. *constant . . . proof*] a version of the proverb 'Time brings the truth to light'.

81–2. *The guilt . . . danger*] i.e. 'I will stand surety for the two gentlemen'.

[*To Somerton*] Come, fear not, sir. Nor judge nor
   evidence
Can bind him o'er who's freed by conscience.
Somerton. Mine stands so upright to the middle zone
   It takes no shadow to't, it goes alone.   *Exeunt.*

88–9.] 'My conscience is clear and walks without a shadow, as if I were in the tropics [*middle zone*] where the sun is directly overhead.'

Act 4

Enter OLD BANKS *and two or three* Countrymen.

Old Banks. My horse this morning runs most piteously of the
glanders, whose nose yesternight was as clean as any
man's here now coming from the barber's. And this, I'll
take my death upon't, is long of this jadish witch, Mother
Sawyer.   5

First Countryman. I took my wife and a servingman in our
town of Edmonton thrashing in my barn together such
corn as country wenches carry to market. And examining
my polecat why she did so, she swore in her conscience
she was bewitched, and what witch have we about us but   10
Mother Sawyer?

Second Countryman. Rid the town of her, else all our wives
will do nothing else but dance about other country
maypoles.

Third Countryman. Our cattle fall, our wives fall, our daugh-   15
ters fall and maidservants fall; and we ourselves shall not
be able to stand if this beast be suffered to graze amongst
us.

---

2. *glanders*] a contagious disease in horses, the chief symptoms of which
are swellings beneath the jaw and discharge of mucous matter from the
nostrils.

4. *take my death*] stake my life.

long of] because of, on account of. (Also in l. 68.)

jadish] ill-tempered.

6. *took*] caught, found.

7. *thrashing*] literally, threshing cereal with a flail to separate seed from
husks (also carrying the meaning 'to copulate with').

9. *polecat*] i.e. whore.

14. *maypoles*] poles decked with ribbons around which merry-makers
danced on May-day (here carrying sexual overtones).

15–17.] 'fall', 'stand' and 'graze' all carry sexual connotations.

Enter W. HAMLUC, *with thatch and link.*

Hamluc. Burn the witch, the witch, the witch, the witch!
All. What hast got there?   20
Hamluc. A handful of thatch plucked off a hovel of hers; and
    they say, when 'tis burning, if she be a witch she'll come
    running in.
Old Banks. Fire it, fire it! I'll stand between thee and home for
    any danger.   25

As that burns, enter the Witch [ELIZABETH SAWYER].

Elizabeth Sawyer. Diseases, plagues, the curse of an old
    woman follow and fall upon you!
All. Are you come, you old trot?
Old Banks. You hot whore, must we fetch you with fire in
    your tail?   30
First Countryman. This thatch is as good as a jury to prove she
    is a witch.
All. Out, witch! Beat her, kick her, set fire on her!
Elizabeth Sawyer. Shall I be murdered by a bed of serpents?
    Help, help!   35

Enter SIR ARTHUR CLARINGTON *and a* Justice.

All. Hang her, beat her, kill her!
Justice. How now? Forbear this violence!
Elizabeth Sawyer. A crew of villains, a knot of bloody hang-
    men set to torment me, I know not why.
Justice. Alas, Neighbour Banks, are you a ringleader in mis-   40
    chief? Fie! To abuse an aged woman!

18.1. W. *HAMLUC*] See note on Actors' Names, l. 6.
link] torch.

21–3.] a common superstition at the time and a feature of the source
material. Goodcole's scepticism as to the validity of such belief and practice
(see Appendix, p. 137) is transferred to the Justice at l. 48.

28. *trot*] beldam, hag, bawd.

29–30.] Old Banks's accusations of Sawyer's sexual insatiability ('hot
whore' and 'fire in your tail') articulate the stereotypical view of women
propagated by many witchcraft persecutors.

34. *bed*] nest.

35.1. a *Justice*] a local Justice of the Peace, a law officer appointed to judge
petty crimes.

37. *Forbear*] stop.

38. *knot*] gang.

Old Banks. Woman? A she-hellcat, a witch! To prove her one,
    we no sooner set fire on the thatch of her house, but in
    she came running as if the devil had sent her in a barrel
    of gunpowder; which trick as surely proves her a witch as   45
    the pox in a snuffling nose is a sign a man is a whore-
    master.

Justice. Come, come. Firing her thatch? Ridiculous! Take
    heed, sirs, what you do. Unless your proofs come better
    armed, instead of turning her into a witch, you'll prove   50
    yourselves stark fools.

All. Fools?

Justice. Arrant fools.

Old Banks. Pray, Master Justice What-do-you-call-'um, hear
    me but in one thing. This grumbling devil owes me, I   55
    know, no good will ever since I fell out with her.

Elizabeth Sawyer. And breakest my back with beating me.

Old Banks. I'll break it worse.

Elizabeth Sawyer. Wilt thou?

Justice. You must not threaten her; 'tis against law. Go on.   60

Old Banks. So, sir, ever since, having a dun cow tied up in my
    backside, let me go thither or but cast mine eye at her,
    and, if I should be hanged, I cannot choose, though it be
    ten times in an hour, but run to the cow and, taking up
    her tail, kiss, saving your worship's reverence, my cow   65
    behind, that the whole town of Edmonton has been ready
    to bepiss themselves with laughing me to scorn.

Justice. And this is long of her?

Old Banks. Who the devil else? For is any man such an ass to
    be such a baby if he were not bewitched?   70

---

46. *pox . . . nose*] a reference to the symptoms of syphilis.

61–7.] It is likely that Gifford's *A Dialogue Concerning Witches and
Witchcrafts* (1593) is the source of Banks's anecdote: 'A third man came in,
and he said she [a witch] was once angry with him, he had a dun cow which
was tied up in a house, for it was winter, he feared that some evil would
follow, and for his life he could not come in where she was, but he must
needs take up her tail and kiss under it' (sig. 1.4v). Sir Arthur's response and
the Justice's admonishment reflect Gifford's sceptical attitude to witch belief.

61. *dun*] brownish-grey.

62. *backside*] backyard.

65. *saving . . . reverence*] a common phrase, apologising for a remark that
might seem disrespectful.

Sir Arthur. Nay, if she be a witch, and the harms she does end
    in such sports, she may 'scape burning.
Justice. Go, go; pray vex her not. She is a subject, and you
    must not be judges of the law to strike her as you please.
All. No, no, we'll find cudgel enough to strike her.   75
Old Banks. Ay, no lips to kiss but my cow's ——!
                Exeunt [OLD BANKS *and* Countrymen].
Elizabeth Sawyer. Rots and foul maladies eat up thee and
    thine!
Justice. Here's none now, Mother Sawyer, but this gentle-
    man, myself and you. Let us to some mild questions;   80
    have you mild answers? Tell us honestly and with a free
    confession—we'll do our best to wean you from it—are
    you a witch or no?
Elizabeth Sawyer. I am none!
Justice. Be not so furious.   85
Elizabeth Sawyer. I am none. None but base curs so bark at
    me. I am none. Or would I were! If every poor old woman
    be trod on thus by slaves, reviled, kicked, beaten, as I am
    daily, she, to be revenged, had need turn witch.
Sir Arthur. And you, to be revenged, have sold your soul to th'   90
    devil.
Elizabeth Sawyer. Keep thine own from him.
Justice. You are too saucy and too bitter.
Elizabeth Sawyer. Saucy? By what commission can he send
    my soul on the devil's errand more than I can his? Is he   95
    a landlord of my soul to thrust it, when he list, out of
    door?
Justice. Know whom you speak to?
Elizabeth Sawyer. A man; perhaps no man. Men in gay
    clothes, whose backs are laden with titles and honours,   100

---

    72. *she may 'scape burning*] In England the punishment for witchcraft was
hanging, not burning. In most witch trials the accused were indicted for
murder or attempted murder by witchcraft.

    75.] i.e. 'No, we won't strike her, our cudgels will'.

    76. *cow's* —— *!*] The quarto's blank implies perhaps that the actor would
have supplied the meaning with a gesture.

    93. *saucy*] presumptuous.

    94. *commission*] authority.

    96. *list*] wishes.

are within far more crooked than I am, and if I be a witch,
more witch-like.

Sir Arthur. You're a base hell-hound.—And now, sir, let me
tell you, far and near she's bruited for a woman that
maintains a spirit that sucks her.   105

Elizabeth Sawyer. I defy thee.

Sir Arthur. Go, go. I can, if need be, bring an hundred voices,
e'en here in Edmonton, that shall loud proclaim thee for
a secret and pernicious witch.

Elizabeth Sawyer. Ha, ha!   110

Justice. Do you laugh? Why laugh you?

Elizabeth Sawyer. At my name, the brave name this knight
gives me—witch!

Justice. Is the name of witch so pleasing to thine ear?

Sir Arthur. Pray, sir, give way, and let her tongue gallop on.   115

Elizabeth Sawyer. A witch! Who is not?
    Hold not that universal name in scorn then.
    What are your painted things in princes' courts,
    Upon whose eyelids lust sits, blowing fires
    To burn men's souls in sensual hot desires,   120
    Upon whose naked paps a lecher's thought
    Acts sin in fouler shapes than can be wrought?

Justice. But those work not as you do.

Elizabeth Sawyer.   No, but far worse.
    These by enchantments can whole lordships change

---

101. *within*] i.e. in their souls.

104. *bruited for*] openly reported to be.

107. *voices*] witnesses.

116–47.] Elizabeth Sawyer's remarks, expressed in a manner outside her
normal register, articulate a range of social criticism which is not uncommon
in the drama of the period. The dramatists generate some sympathy for her
plight by providing such comment.

118. *painted things*] women who beautify themselves with cosmetics; cf.
Hamlet, 5.1.186, 'Now get you to my lady's chamber and tell her, let her paint
an inch thick'.

121. *paps*] breasts.

123–32.] Sawyer's comments are in the tradition of satirical attacks on
Jacobean conspicuous consumption as exemplified in a wide range of dramatic work; see, for example, Middleton or Tourneur, *The Revenger's Tragedy*, 3.5.74–5, 'Are lordships sold to maintain ladyships / For the poor benefit
of a bewitching minute'.

124. *lordships*] estates.

To trunks of rich attire, turn ploughs and teams   125
To Flanders mares and coaches, and huge trains
Of servitors to a French butterfly.
Have you not city-witches who can turn
Their husbands' wares, whole standing shops of wares,
To sumptuous tables, gardens of stol'n sin;   130
In one year wasting what scarce twenty win?
Are not these witches?
Justice.   Yes, yes; but the law
Casts not an eye on these.
Elizabeth Sawyer.   Why then on me
Or any lean old beldam? Reverence once
Had wont to wait on age. Now an old woman   135
Ill-favoured grown with years, if she be poor
Must be called bawd or witch. Such so abused
Are the coarse witches, t'other are the fine,
Spun for the devil's own wearing.
Sir Arthur.   And so is thine.
Elizabeth Sawyer. She on whose tongue a whirlwind sits to
        blow   140
A man out of himself, from his soft pillow
To lean his head on rocks and fighting waves,
Is not that scold a witch? The man of law
Whose honeyed hopes the credulous client draws,

---

126. *Flanders mares*] heavy and powerful horses used to draw carriages.

127. *servitors*] male servants.

French butterfly] a vain or gaudily attired person, often a courtier, having affected French manners or clothes.

128–9. *turn . . . wares*] i.e. convert and squander the profits of their husbands' businesses.

130. *gardens*] Gardens and garden-houses were often used for immoral purposes; see, for example, Shakespeare, *Measure for Measure*, 4.1.27–32 and Gordon Williams, *A Dictionary of Sexual Language and Imagery in Shakespearean and Stuart Literature* (1994).

131. *what . . . win*] what can scarcely be earned in twenty years.

134–5. *Reverence . . . age*] i.e. 'The elderly used to be treated with respect'.

135–7. *Now . . . witch*] The presentation of Elizabeth Sawyer parallels Scot's sympathy and scepticism in *Discovery of Witchcraft* (1584): 'One sort of such as are said to be witches, are women which be commonly old, lame, blear-eyed, foul, and full of wrinkles; poor, sullen, superstitious, and papists' (I.3).

143. *scold*] nagging woman.

As bees by tinkling basins, to swarm to him   145
From his own hive to work the wax in his;
He is no witch, not he!
Sir Arthur.   But these men-witches
Are not in trading with hell's merchandise
Like such as you are, that for a word, a look,
Denial of a coal of fire, kill men,   150
Children and cattle.
Elizabeth Sawyer.   Tell them, sir, that do so.
Am I accused for such an one?
Sir Arthur.   Yes, 'twill be sworn.
Elizabeth Sawyer. Dare any swear I ever tempted maiden,
With golden hooks flung at her chastity,
To come and lose her honour, and, being lost,   155
To pay not a denier for't? Some slaves have done it.
Men-witches can, without the fangs of law
Drawing once one drop of blood, put counterfeit pieces
Away for true gold.
Sir Arthur.   By one thing she speaks
I know now she's a witch, and dare no longer   160
Hold conference with the fury.
Justice.   Let's then away.—
Old woman, mend thy life, get home and pray.
          Exeunt [SIR ARTHUR CLARINGTON *and* Justice].
Elizabeth Sawyer. For his confusion.

Enter DOG.

                    My dear Tom-boy, welcome!
I am torn in pieces by a pack of curs
Clapped all upon me, and for want of thee.   165

145–6. *As . . . his*] It was a popular belief that swarms of bees could be
hived or reclaimed by beating pans and basins, but such action may have
merely been a means of claiming ownership of the swarm.

156. *denier*] a small French coin of very little value.

159–61. *By . . . fury*] Sir Arthur takes it that Elizabeth Sawyer has divined
by supernatural means his relationship with Winnifride. It was sometimes
believed that witches had such powers, but it is Sir Arthur's guilt which is
stressed here, since Sawyer's comment is general and does not seem to be
directed towards him.

163. *his confusion*] Sir Arthur's ruin.

165. *Clapped*] pounced.

Comfort me; thou shalt have the teat anon.

Dog. Bow, wow! I'll have it now.

Elizabeth Sawyer.   I am dried up
     With cursing and with madness, and have yet
     No blood to moisten these sweet lips of thine.
     Stand on thy hind-legs up. Kiss me, my Tommy,   170
     And rub away some wrinkles on my brow
     By making my old ribs to shrug for joy
     Of thy fine tricks. What hast thou done? Let's tickle.
                                   [*They embrace.*]
     Hast thou struck the horse lame as I bid thee?

Dog. Yes, and nipped the sucking child.

Elizabeth Sawyer.   Ho, ho, my dainty,   175
     My little pearl! No lady loves her hound,
     Monkey or parakeet, as I do thee.

Dog. The maid has been churning butter nine hours, but it
     shall not come.

Elizabeth Sawyer. Let 'em eat cheese and choke.

Dog.   I had rare sport   180
     Among the clowns i'th'morris.

Elizabeth Sawyer.   I could dance
     Out of my skin to hear thee. But, my curl-pate,
     That jade, that foul-tongued whore, Nan Ratcliffe,
     Who, for a little soap licked by my sow,

---

173. *fine tricks*] The 'tricks' which the Dog has performed recall many of the complaints made against witches.

tickle] used variously for sexual activity in Renaissance texts. It is unclear what is intended here, but the text calls for Dog, disturbingly like a human lover, to stand on his hind legs. The dramatists may, however, have intended more innocent intimacies. In the 1981 RSC production the characters rolled on the floor together, whilst in the Bristol production (1984) Elizabeth Sawyer tickled the Dog's stomach.

175. *nipped*] snatched away.

sucking] suckling.

176. *pearl*] a common pet name for a dog.

180. *rare*] excellent.

182. *curl-pate*] affectionate address to the dog, i.e. curly-headed one.

183. *jade*] a term of contempt applied to a woman.

184. *soap*] This detail is taken from Goodcole: 'She was also indicted for that she, the said Elizabeth Sawyer, by diabolical help and out of her malice aforethought, did witch unto death Agnes Ratcliefe, a neighbour of hers dwelling in the town of Edmonton where she did likewise dwell, and the

Struck and almost had lamed it; did not I charge thee   185
To pinch that quean to th'heart?

Dog. Bow, wow, wow! Look here else.

Enter ANNE RATCLIFFE *mad.*

Anne Ratcliffe. See, see, see! The Man i'th'Moon has built a
new windmill, and what running there's from all quarters
of the city to learn the art of grinding.   190

Elizabeth Sawyer. Ho, ho, ho! I thank thee, my sweet
mongrel.

Anne Ratcliffe. Hoyda! A pox of the devil's false hopper! All
the golden meal runs into the rich knaves' purses, and the
poor have nothing but bran. Hey derry down! Are not   195
you Mother Sawyer?

Elizabeth Sawyer. No, I am a lawyer.

Anne Ratcliffe. Art thou! I prithee let me scratch thy face, for
thy pen has flayed off a great many men's skins. You'll
have brave doings in the vacation, for knaves and fools   200
are at variance in every village. I'll sue Mother Sawyer,
and her own sow shall give in evidence against her.

Elizabeth Sawyer. [*To Dog*] Touch her.

[*Dog touches Anne Ratcliffe.*]

---

cause that urged her thereunto was because that Agnes Ratcleife did strike a
sow of hers in her sight for licking up a little soap where she had laid it, and
for that Elizabeth Sawyer would be revenged of her and thus threatened
Agnes Ratcleife that it should be a dear blow unto her, which accordingly fell
out and suddenly' (p. 138). It is possible that by 'soap', 'sop' is intended.

186. *pinch . . . heart*] kill that hussy, loose woman.

189. *windmill*] a cant term for brothel.

190. *the art of grinding*] i.e. the art of grinding corn; with a play on
'extortion' (also meaning 'copulation').

193. *Hoyda!*] exclamation of surprise.

hopper] container through which the corn passes for grinding, also with a
sexual signification.

195. *Hey derry down*] a refrain of a song, the singing of which is used to
indicate madness as in the manner of Ophelia in Shakespeare's *Hamlet*.

198. *let . . . face*] It was widely believed that a witch's *maleficium* could be
removed by drawing her blood and particularly by scratching her face.

200. *brave doings*] good business.

in the vacation] between legal terms when lawyers returned to the country.

203.1.] Although quarto provides no SD, Anne Ratcliffe's response at l.
204 suggests that Dog has carried out Sawyer's command and touched her in
some way. Cf. G. B. Harrison (ed.), *The Trial of the Lancashire Witches, A.D.*

Anne Ratcliffe. Oh, my ribs are made of a paned hose, and
    they break. There's a Lancashire hornpipe in my throat.   205
    Hark how it tickles it, with doodle, doodle, doodle,
    doodle! Welcome, sergeants! Welcome, devil! Hands,
    hands! Hold hands and dance around, around, around.

       Enter OLD BANKS, *his son* [YOUNG BANKS] *the Clown,*
           OLD RATCLIFFE [*and*] Country-fellows.

Old Ratcliffe. She's here. Alas, my poor wife is here!
Old Banks. Catch her fast, and have her into some close   210
    chamber, do, for she's as many wives are, stark mad.
Young Banks. The witch, Mother Sawyer! The witch, the
    devil!
Old Ratcliffe. Oh, my dear wife! Help, sirs!
    [OLD RATCLIFFE *and the* Country-fellows] *carry her off.*
Old Banks. You see your work, Mother Bumby.   215
Elizabeth Sawyer. My work? Should she and all you here run
    mad, is the work mine?

MDCXII (1929), p. 69, 'the said Spirit *Dandy* appeared unto this Examinate,
and said, Thou didst touch the said *Duckworth*; whereunto this Examinate
answered, he did not touch him: yes (said the spirit again) thou didst touch
him, and therefore I have power of him: whereupon this Examinate joined
with the said Spirit, and then wished the said Spirit to kill the said *Duckworth*:
and within one week, then next after, *Duckworth* died.' See also 2.1.160–73.
    204. *paned hose*] breeches made in panes or strips, or in pleats which
parted slightly, showing a rich lining and which were liable to break at the
seams.
    205. *Lancashire hornpipe*] a wind instrument said to have been so called
from having the bell and mouthpiece made of horn. Lancashire had a
reputation for witchcraft due to the witch epidemic of 1612. In addition the
phrase has sexual connotations, Lancashire men being noted for their sexual
prowess (see Williams), which are continued with 'tickles' and 'doodle,
doodle'.
    210. *have*] convey.
    close] secure.
    214.1.] Some editors have the Dog leave the stage at this point, returning
at l. 270, but there seems no good reason for this; indeed the presence of the
Dog during the intervening action serves to increase the ironic tension. In the
1981 RSC production the Dog observed the subsequent events from the top
of a notch post.
    215. *Mother Bumby*] the heroine of Lyly's comedy (1594), who was a wise
woman rather than a witch.

Young Banks. No, on my conscience, she would not hurt a
devil of two years old.

Enter OLD RATCLIFFE *and the rest.*

How now! What's become of her?   220
Old Ratcliffe. Nothing. She's become nothing but the miser-
able trunk of a wretched woman. We were in her hands as
reeds in a mighty tempest. Spite of our strengths away she
brake, and nothing in her mouth being heard but 'the
devil, the witch, the witch, the devil', she beat out her   225
own brains, and so died.
Young Banks. It's any man's case, be he never so wise, to die
when his brains go a-wool-gathering.
Old Banks. Masters, be ruled by me, let's all to a justice.—
Hag, thou hast done this, and thou shalt answer it.   230
Elizabeth Sawyer. Banks, I defy thee.
Old Banks. Get a warrant first to examine her, then ship her
to Newgate. Here's enough, if all her other villainies were
pardoned, to burn her for a witch.—You have a spirit,
they say, comes to you in the likeness of a dog; we shall   235
see your cur at one time or other. If we do, unless it be the
devil himself, he shall go howling to the gaol in one chain,
and thou in another.
Elizabeth Sawyer. Be hanged thou in a third, and do thy
worst!   240
Young Banks. How, father! You send the poor dumb thing
howling to th'gaol? He that makes him howl makes me
roar.
Old Banks. Why, foolish boy, dost thou know him?

218–19. *she . . . old*] an allusion to the proverb, 'There's no more harm in
him than in a devil of two years old'.

228. *brains go a-wool-gathering*] Proverbial, 'His wits go a woolgathering'.

232. *examine*] interrogate.

ship] convey.

233. *Newgate*] Elizabeth Sawyer was imprisoned in Newgate Prison,
where Goodcole was, according to the title-page of his pamphlet, her continual visitor.

234. *burn . . . witch*] See note to l. 72 above.

242–3. *He . . . roar*] i.e. 'Anyone who makes Dog suffer causes me to cry
out'. (Young Banks has developed an absurd affection for Dog, and doesn't
want to see him arrested.)

Young Banks. No matter if I do or not. He's bailable, I am   245
sure, by law. But if the dog's word will not be taken, mine
shall.

Old Banks. Thou bail for a dog?

Young Banks. Yes, or a bitch either, being my friend. I'll lie by
the heels myself before Puppison shall; his dog-days are   250
not come yet, I hope.

Old Banks. What manner of dog is it? Didst ever see him?

Young Banks. See him? Yes, and given him a bone to gnaw
twenty times. The dog is no court-foisting hound that fills
his belly full by base wagging his tail. Neither is it a   255
citizen's water-spaniel, enticing his master to go a-
ducking twice or thrice a week whilst his wife makes
ducks and drakes at home. This is no Paris-garden
bandog neither, that keeps a bow-wow-wowing to have
butchers bring their curs thither, and when all comes to   260
all they run away like sheep. Neither is this the Black
Dog of Newgate.

Old Banks. No, Goodman Son-fool, but the dog of hell-gate.

Young Banks. I say, Goodman Father-fool, it's a lie.

All. He's bewitched.   265

Young Banks. A gross lie as big as myself. The devil in St

249–50. *lie . . . heels*] i.e. in irons or in the stocks.

250. *Puppison*] probably equivalent to 'his puppyship'.

dog-days] an expression used for the hottest and most unwholesome time
of the year, which was reputed to drive dogs mad. See 3.1.108 and note.

254. *court-foisting hound*] i.e. flattering court dog; spaniels were noted for
their fawning.

256–8. *water-spaniel . . . home*] i.e. a retrieving dog who encourages his
citizen owner out hunting whilst his wife misbehaves at home. Cf. the
proverb, 'To make ducks and drakes with one's money'.

258–9. *Paris-garden bandog*] mastiff or bloodhound used in bear-baiting at
the Bear Garden at Paris Garden on Bankside, Southwark.

261–2. *Black Dog of Newgate*] the legendary spectral dog who haunted the
prison at execution time and figures in Thomas Dekker's *English Villainies
Discovered by Lantern and Candlelight* (1608) and also provides the title of a
poem and essay by Luke Hutton (1600) and a lost play (1602).

263. *Goodman*] a common form of address for yeoman and farmers.

dog of hell-gate] Cerberus.

266–7. *The devil in St Dunstan's*] a reference to the Devil Tavern near
Temple Bar and St Dunstan's Church in Fleet Street. Its sign represented St
Dunstan pulling the devil's nose with his pincers.

Dunstan's will as soon drink with this poor cur as with
any Temple-bar laundress that washes and wrings
lawyers.

Dog. Bow, wow, wow, wow!   270

All. Oh, the dog's here, the dog's here!

Old Banks. It was the voice of a dog.

Young Banks. The voice of a dog? If that voice were a dog's,
what voice had my mother? So am I a dog; bow, wow,
wow! It was I that barked so, father, to make coxcombs of   275
these clowns.

Old Banks. However, we'll be coxcombed no longer; away,
therefore, to th'justice for a warrant, and then, Gammer
Gurton, have at your needle of witchcraft!

Elizabeth Sawyer. And prick thine own eyes out. Go, peevish   280
fools!

    Exeunt [OLD BANKS, OLD RATCLIFFE *and* Countrymen].

Young Banks. Ningle, you had like to have spoiled all with
your bowings. I was glad to put 'em off with one of my
dog-tricks on a sudden. I am bewitched, little cost-
me-nought, to love thee—a pox, that morris makes me   285
spit in thy mouth. I dare not stay. Farewell, Ningle,
you whoreson dog's nose. Farewell, witch.   *Exit.*

Dog. Bow, wow, wow, wow.

Elizabeth Sawyer. Mind him not, he's not worth thy worrying.
Run at a fairer game, that foul-mouthed knight, scurvy   290
Sir Arthur. Fly at him, my Tommy, and pluck out's
throat.

---

268. *Temple-bar laundress*] Laundresses had a reputation for easy virtue,
and so 'washes' and 'wrings' may have bawdy overtones.

270. *Bow . . . wow!*] In Goodcole Elizabeth Sawyer is reported as saying
that the dog's barking indicated that he accomplished the mischief that she
bid him do; see Appendix, p. 144.

278–9. *Gammer Gurton*] a reference to the title figure in the comedy
Gammer Gurton's Needle (1557) who, although old and irascible, has no links
to witchcraft.

279. *have at*] i.e. beware, guard carefully.

282. *you . . . have*] you nearly.

283. *bowings*] barking.

284–5. *cost-me-nought*] used as a term of endearment.

286. *spit in thy mouth*] i.e. 'do you a favour'; literally, a gesture of affection
which was believed to please dogs.

289. *Mind him not*] Pay no attention to him (Old Banks).

Dog. No, there's a dog already biting's — his conscience.

Elizabeth Sawyer. That's a sure bloodhound. Come, let's
    home and play.   295

    Our black work ended, we'll make holiday.   *Exeunt.*

4.2

            Enter KATHERINE; *a bed thrust forth, on it*
                FRANK [THORNEY] *in a slumber.*

Katherine. Brother, brother! So sound asleep? That's well.

Frank Thorney. No, not I, sister. He that's wounded here,
    As I am; all my other hurts are bitings
    Of a poor flea; but he that here once bleeds
    Is maimed incurably.

Katherine.   My good sweet brother,   5
    For now my sister must grow up in you,
    Though her loss strikes you through, and that I feel
    The blow as deep, I pray thee be not cruel
    To kill me too by seeing you cast away
    In your own helpless sorrow. Good love, sit up,   10
    And if you can give physic to yourself,
    I shall be well.

Frank Thorney.   I'll do my best.

Katherine.   I thank you.
    What do you look about for?

Frank Thorney.   Nothing, nothing;
    But I was thinking, sister.

293.] i.e. 'His conscience is the dog which is biting him'. Gifford's emendation has been adopted here because it clarifies quarto's 'biting's conscience'.

0.1. thrust forth] i.e. thrust downstage. This was a common stage practice; cf. *Thomas of Woodstock*, and Shakespeare's *Henry VI, Pt 2* and *Othello*.

  1. *Brother*] i.e. brother-in-law.

  2. *sister*] i.e. sister-in-law.

  here] i.e. in the heart.

  3–4. *all . . . flea*] Proverbial, 'It is but a flea-biting'.

  6.] i.e. 'for now you must replace my dead sister in my affections'.

  7. *through*] thoroughly, deeply.

  11. *physic*] medicine.

Katherine.   Dear heart, what?

Frank Thorney. Who but a fool would thus be bound to a bed   15
    Having this room to walk in?

Katherine.   Why do you talk so?
    Would you were fast asleep.

Frank Thorney.   No, no; I'm not idle.
    But here's my meaning: being robbed as I am,
    Why should my soul, which married was to hers,
    Live in divorce, and not fly after her?   20
    Why should not I walk hand in hand with death
    To find my love out?

Katherine.   That were well, indeed,
    Your time being come. When death is sent to call you,
    No doubt you shall meet her.

Frank Thorney.   Why should not I go
    Without calling?

Katherine.   Yes, brother, so you might,   25
    Were there no place to go to when you're gone
    But only this.

Frank Thorney.   Troth, sister, thou sayst true,
    For when a man has been an hundred years
    Hard travelling o'er the tottering bridge of age,
    He's not the thousand part upon his way.   30
    All life is but a wandering to find home.
    When we are gone, we are there. Happy were man
    Could here his voyage end; he should not then
    Answer how well or ill he steered his soul
    By heaven's or by hell's compass; how he put in,   35
    Losing blessed goodness' shore, at such a sin;
    Nor how life's dear provision he has spent;
    Nor how far he in's navigation went
    Beyond commission. This were a fine reign,
    To do ill and not hear of it again.   40

---

17. *idle*] delirious.
26–7. *Were . . . this*] i.e. if you could just die and not go to eternal damnation in hell.
32. *When . . . there*] i.e. 'When we die, we enter eternal life'.
35. *put in*] i.e. steered his ship into the harbour.
39. *commission*] authority, what is permitted.

Yet then were man more wretched than a beast,
For, sister, our dead pay is sure the best.
Katherine. 'Tis so, the best or worst, and I wish heaven
To pay—and so I know it will—that traitor,
That devil Somerton, who stood in mine eye   45
Once as an angel, home to his deservings.
What villain but himself, once loving me,
With Warbeck's soul would pawn his own to hell
To be revenged on my poor sister?
Frank Thorney.   Slaves!
A pair of merciless slaves! Speak no more of them.   50
Katherine. I think this talking hurts you.
Frank Thorney.   Does me no good, I'm sure.
I pay for't everywhere.
Katherine.   I have done then.
Eat, if you cannot sleep. You have these two days
Not tasted any food.—Jane, is it ready?
Frank Thorney. What's ready? What's ready?   55

[*Enter a* Maid *with chicken.*]

Katherine. I have made ready a roasted chicken for you.
Sweet, wilt thou eat?
Frank Thorney.   A pretty stomach on a sudden; yes—
There's one in the house can play upon a lute,
Good girl, let's hear him too.
Katherine.   You shall, dear brother.
                              [*Exit* Maid.]
Would I were a musician, you should hear   60
How I would feast your ear.   *Lute plays.*
                    Stay, mend your pillow
And raise you higher.
Frank Thorney.   I am up too high,
Am I not, sister, now?
Katherine.   No, no, 'tis well,

---

42. *dead pay*] reward after death.
44–6.] i.e. to punish utterly and deservedly that devil, Somerton, whom I
once thought well of.
48.] i.e. would, in league with Warbeck, sell his soul to the devil.
57. *A pretty . . . sudden*] i.e. 'I have a sudden appetite'.
61. *mend*] plump up.

Fall to, fall to.—A knife. Here's never a knife,
Brother, I'll look out yours.   [*She picks up his coat.*]

   Enter DOG, *shrugging as it were for joy, and dances.*

Frank Thorney.   Sister, O sister,   65
   I am ill upon a sudden and can eat nothing.
Katherine. In very deed you shall. The want of food
   Makes you so faint. [*She discovers a knife.*] Ha! Here's
      none in your pocket.
   I'll go fetch a knife.   *Exit.*
Frank Thorney.   Will you? 'Tis well, all's well.

She gone, he searches first one, then the other pocket. Knife found.
DOG *runs off. He lies on one side. The* Spirit *of* SUSAN *his second
wife comes to the bedside. He stares at it, and turning to the other
side, it's there too. In the meantime,* WINNIFRIDE *as a page comes
in, stands at his bed's feet sadly. He, frighted, sits upright. The*
                      Spirit *vanishes.*

---

65. SD] The Dog's entrance and joyful behaviour emphasise the devil's
influence in Frank Thorney's fate. It is significant that he exits as soon as the
crime is discovered.

68. SD] Although the quarto text provides no SD it is clear from ll. 115–
18 below that Katherine discovers the knife but immediately dissimulates. It
is possible to stage the text so that the Dog puts the knife in Frank's pocket
(having retrieved it when tying Frank's arms at 3.3.71) as in the RSC 1981
production where he lurked under Frank's bed until his black arm leaned out
to slip the incriminating bloody knife into Frank's jacket pocket where
Katherine could find it. Alternatively, Frank could have pocketed the knife
after the murder and his refusal of food at 4.2.66, could be provoked by fear
that the knife will be discovered and thus reveal his guilt.

69.1–6.] The quarto's stage-direction appears to describe stage business
which takes place over a number of lines; for example Frank's exclamation
'On this side now!' (l. 75) seems to be a response to the appearance of
Susan's Spirit on the other side of the bed. It is possible that the Spirit does
not exit until Winnifride's speech at l. 80. Alternatively, if the stage direction
is to be understood to indicate that Winnifride enters after the Spirit has
vanished, Frank's subsequent reaction must be understood as his shocked
confusion in the wake of the apparition.

69.2. *Spirit* of *SUSAN*] The nature of the Spirit is ambiguous. Since Susan
died forgiving Frank Thorney, it is unlikely that it is her ghost returning to
torment him. It has been suggested that it might be interpreted as an
impersonating devil managed by the Dog. Frank subsequently suggests that
it was a figment of his imagination (ll. 84–5). In any event the Spirit's
entrance heightens the dramatic pathos of the scene.

Frank Thorney. What art thou?
Winnifride.   A lost creature.
Frank Thorney.   So am I too.—   70
      Win? Ah, my she-page!
Winnifride.   For your sake I put on
      A shape that's false, yet do I wear a heart
      True to you as your own.
Frank Thorney.   Would mine and thine
      Were fellows in one house! Kneel by me here.
      On this side now! How darst thou come to mock me   75
      On both sides of my bed?
Winnifride.   When?
Frank Thorney.   But just now;
      Outface me, stare upon me with strange postures,
      Turn my soul wild by a face in which were drawn
      A thousand ghosts leapt newly from their graves
      To pluck me into a winding-sheet.
Winnifride.   Believe it,   80
      I came no nearer to you than yon place
      At your bed's feet, and of the house had leave,
      Calling myself your horse-boy, in to come
      And visit my sick master.
Frank Thorney.   Then 'twas my fancy,
      Some windmill in my brains for want of sleep.   85
Winnifride. Would I might never sleep so you could rest.
      But you have plucked a thunder on your head,
      Whose noise cannot cease suddenly. Why should you
      Dance at the wedding of a second wife,
      When scarce the music which you heard at mine   90
      Had ta'en a farewell of you? Oh, this was ill!
      And they who thus can give both hands away
      In th'end shall want their best limbs.
Frank Thorney.   Winnifride,

---

72. *shape*] appearance, disguise.
80. *winding-sheet*] shroud, burial sheet; ghosts commonly announce impending deaths in plays of the period; see *The White Devil*, 5.4.123.1–3 (Revels ed.).
82. *of . . . leave*] i.e. with the family's permission.
85. *Some . . . sleep*] Proverbial, 'He has windmills in his head'.

The chamber-door fast?

Winnifride.   Yes.

Frank Thorney.   Sit thee then down,
And when thou'st heard me speak, melt into tears.   95
Yet I, to save those eyes of thine from weeping,
Being to write a story of us two,
Instead of ink, dipped my sad pen in blood;
When of thee I took leave, I went abroad
Only for pillage, as a freebooter,   100
What gold soe'er I got to make it thine.
To please a father I have heaven displeased.
Striving to cast two wedding rings in one,
Through my bad workmanship I now have none;
I have lost her and thee.

Winnifride.   I know she's dead,   105
But you have me still.

Frank Thorney.   Nay, her this hand
Murdered, and so I lose thee too.

Winnifride.   Oh, me!

Frank Thorney. Be quiet, for thou my evidence art,
Jury and judge. Sit quiet and I'll tell all.

> *As they whisper, enter at one end of the stage* OLD
> CARTER *and* KATHERINE, DOG *at the other, pawing*
> *softly at* FRANK [THORNEY].

Katherine. [*To Old Carter*] I have run madding up and down
to find you,   110
Being laden with the heaviest news that ever
Poor daughter carried.

Old Carter.   Why? Is the boy dead?

Katherine. Dead, sir! Oh, father, we are cozened. You are told
The murderer sings in prison, and he laughs here.

---

100. *freebooter*] one who goes in search of plunder.

109.2. DOG . . . softly] Once again the Dog enters to witness the revelation of Frank's Thorney's guilt. The Dog's pawing of Frank suggests that he claims him for his own.

110. *madding*] frenziedly.

113. *cozened*] deceived.

114. *murderer . . . prison*] It was commonly thought that a prisoner sang just before death.

This villain killed my sister. See else, see,   115
    [*Showing the knife in* FRANK THORNEY'S *coat-pocket.*]
    A bloody knife in's pocket.
Old Carter.   Bless me, patience!
Frank Thorney. The knife, the knife, the knife!
Katherine. What knife?   *Exit* DOG.
Frank Thorney.   To cut my chicken up, my chicken.
    Be you my carver, father.
Old Carter.   That I will.
Katherine. [*Aside*] How the devil steels our brows after
    doing ill!   120
Frank Thorney. My stomach and my sight are taken from me;
    All is not well within me.
Old Carter. I believe thee, boy; I that have seen so many
    moons clap their horns on other men's foreheads to strike
    them sick, yet mine to 'scape and be well; I that never cast   125
    away a fee upon urinals, but am as sound as an honest
    man's conscience when he's dying, I should cry out as
    thou dost, 'All is not well within me', felt I but the bag of
    thy imposthumes. Ah, poor villain! Ah, my wounded
    rascal! All my grief is, I have now small hope of thee.   130
Frank Thorney. Do the surgeons say my wounds are
    dangerous, then?
Old Carter. Yes, yes and there's no way with thee but one.
Frank Thorney. Would he were to open them!
Old Carter. I'll go to fetch him. I'll make an holiday to see thee
    as I wish.   *Exit to fetch* Officers.   135

---

115. *else*] if it is not believed.

120. *steels our brows*] i.e. hardens our hearts.

123–4. *many . . . foreheads*] Horns usually indicate cuckoldry in plays of
the period, but the implication here is one of madness associated with the
changes of the moon.

126. *urinals*] glass vessels employed to receive urine for medical examination or inspection.

128. *bag*] sack in the body containing poison (*OED* 11).

129. *imposthumes*] swellings or cysts on any part of the body; but here
used figuratively to signify moral corruption.

132. *there's . . . one*] i.e. 'trial and subsequent execution are inevitable for
you'. See the proverb, 'There is no way but one'.

133.] i.e. 'If only the surgeon would open and cleanse my wounds!' With
added meaning of cleansing sins.

134. *I'll make an holiday*] i.e. 'I would rejoice'.

Frank Thorney. A wondrous kind old man.

Winnifride. [*Aside*] Your sin's the blacker so to abuse his
    goodness.

    [*Aloud*] Master, how do you?

Frank Thorney.   Pretty well now, boy.

    I have such odd qualms come 'cross my stomach.

    I'll fall to. Boy, cut me.

Winnifride.   [*Aside*] You have cut me, I'm sure.   140

    [*Aloud.*] A leg or wing, sir?

Frank Thorney.   No, no, no; a wing.

    [*Aside*] Would I had wings but to soar up yon tower.

    But here's a clog that hinders me.

      [*Enter*] *Father* [OLD CARTER] *with her* [SUSAN'S *body*] *in*
        a coffin [*carried by two* Servants].

                    What's that?

Old Carter. That? What? Oh, now I see her; 'tis a young
    wench, my daughter, sirrah, sick to the death, and hear-   145
    ing thee to be an excellent rascal for letting blood, she
    looks out at a casement and cries, 'Help, help! Stay that
    man! Him I must have, or none.'

Frank Thorney. For pity's sake, remove her. See, she stares
    With one broad open eye still in my face.   150

Old Carter. Thou puttest both hers out, like a villain as thou
    art. Yet see, she is willing to lend thee one again to find
    out the murderer, and that's thyself.

Frank Thorney. Old man, thou liest!

Old Carter. So shalt thou, i'th'gaol.—Run for officers.   155

Katherine. Oh, thou merciless slave!

    She was, though yet above ground, in her grave

    To me; but thou hast torn it up again.

    Mine eyes too much drowned, now must feel more rain.

Old Carter. Fetch officers.   160

                    Exit KATHERINE.

137.] Some editors address this line to Frank, but Winnifride's use of
'Master' in the next line suggests that only at this point does she address him.

140. *cut me*] i.e. 'carve for me'; Winnifride picks up Frank's phrase to play
on the meaning 'injured me'.

143. *clog*] block or heavy piece of wood attached to the leg or neck of a
man or beast to prevent escape.

Frank Thorney. For whom?

Old Carter. For thee, sirrah, sirrah! Some knives have foolish
posies upon them, but thine has a villainous one. Look!
Oh, it is enamelled with the heart-blood of thy hated wife,
my beloved daughter. What sayst thou to this evidence?   165
Is't not sharp? Does't not strike home? Thou canst not
answer honestly and without a trembling heart to this one
point, this terrible bloody point.

Winnifride.   I beseech you, sir,
Strike him no more; you see he's dead already.   170

Old Carter. Oh, sir, you held his horses. You are as arrant a
rogue as he. Up, go you too.

Frank Thorney. As you're a man, throw not upon that woman
Your loads of tyranny, for she's innocent.

Old Carter. How! How! A woman? Is't grown to a fashion for   175
women in all countries to wear the breeches?

Winnifride. I am not as my disguise speaks me, sir, his page,
But his first, only wife, his lawful wife.

Old Carter. How! How! More fire i'th'bedstraw!

Winnifride. The wrongs which singly fell upon your daughter   180
On me are multiplied. She lost a life,
But I an husband and myself must lose
If you call him to a bar for what he has done.

Old Carter. He has done it, then?

Winnifride. Yes, 'tis confessed to me.

Frank Thorney.   Dost thou betray me?   185

Winnifride. Oh, pardon me, dear heart! I am mad to lose thee,
And know not what I speak; but if thou didst,

---

162. *sirrah*] contemptuous form of address, usually directed at
underlings.

163. *posies*] short mottoes, originally a line or verse of poetry and usually
in patterned language inscribed on a knife or within a ring, as an heraldic
emblem.

166–8. *sharp . . . strike . . . point*] The 'knife' puns serve to stress Carter's
emotional anguish, which Winnifride responds to by urging him to stop his
verbal attack.

170. *dead*] i.e. mortified.

172. *Up*] i.e. for trial.

179. *More fire i'th'bedstraw*] i.e. 'More concealed mischief'; an allusion to
the proverb, 'It is a dangerous fire begins in the bedstraw'.

183. *bar*] court of law.

I must arraign this father for two sins,
Adultery and murder.

Enter KATHERINE.

Katherine.   Sir, they are come.

Old Carter. Arraign me for what thou wilt, all Middlesex   190
knows me better for an honest man than the middle of a
market-place knows thee for an honest woman. Rise,
sirrah, and don your tacklings; rig yourself for the gallows, or I'll carry thee thither on my back. Your trull shall
to the gaol go with you. There be as fine Newgate birds   195
as she that can draw him in. Pox on's wounds!

Frank Thorney. I have served thee, and my wages now are
      paid,
Yet my worst punishment shall, I hope, be stayed.

Exeunt.

---

188. *arraign*] accuse, charge.

190. *Arraign . . . wilt*] Old Carter takes Winnifride's phrase 'this father' at
at l. 188 to refer to himself, but it is obvious that she is accusing Frank, as the
father of her future child, of adultery and murder.

191–2. *middle . . . market-place*] Carter appears to be referring to the loca-
tion of the pillory in order to expose Winnifride's guilt.

193. *tacklings*] gear, used figuratively here for clothes.

 rig] prepare.

194. *I'll carry . . . back*] possibly an allusion to the traditional image of the
Vice carrying the sinner to hell, depicted in such plays as Wager's *The Longer
Thou Livest, the More Fool Thou Art.*

 trull] concubine, strumpet.

195. *Newgate birds*] prisoners in Newgate Gaol.

197. *served thee*] treated thee (Old Carter) badly.

198. *worst punishment*] damnation, as well as execution.

Act 5

Enter MOTHER [ELIZABETH] SAWYER *alone.*

Elizabeth Sawyer. Still wronged by every slave, and not a dog
　　Bark in his dame's defence? I am called witch,
　　Yet am myself bewitched from doing harm.
　　Have I given up myself to thy black lust
　　Thus to be scorned? Not see me in three days! 　　　　5
　　I'm lost without my Tomalin. Prithee come.
　　Revenge to me is sweeter far than life;
　　Thou art my raven on whose coal-black wings
　　Revenge comes flying to me. Oh, my best love!
　　I am on fire, even in the midst of ice, 　　　　　　10
　　Raking my blood up till my shrunk knees feel
　　Thy curled head leaning on them. Come then,
　　　　my darling!
　　If in the air thou hover'st, fall upon me
　　In some dark cloud; and as I oft have seen
　　Dragons and serpents in the elements, 　　　　　　15
　　Appear thou now so to me. Art thou i'th'sea?
　　Muster up all the monsters from the deep,
　　And be the ugliest of them. So that my bulch
　　Show but his swarth cheek to me, let earth cleave
　　And break from hell, I care not! Could I run 　　　20

---

6. *Tomalin*] affectionate diminutive of Tom.

7.] Cf. the proverb 'Revenge is sweet'.

8–23.] Elizabeth Sawyer's language may seem incongruous for a village witch, but its intensity is dramatically effective in articulating her state of mind. An audience may thus feel sympathy for her situation but also horror at her willingness to destroy the world in order to enjoy the devil as a lover.

8. *raven*] a bird traditionally regarded as an omen of ill-fortune.

18. *bulch*] a rare form of 'bulchin', a bull-calf, used here as a term of endearment.

19. *swarth*] dusky, swarthy.

Like a swift powder-mine beneath the world,
Up would I blow it all to find out thee,
Though I lay ruined in it. Not yet come?
I must then fall to my old prayer,
Sanctibiceter nomen tuum.   25
Not yet come? Worrying of wolves, biting of mad dogs,
the manges and the—

Enter DOG [*now white*].

Dog. How now! Whom art thou cursing?
Elizabeth Sawyer. Thee! Ha! No, 'tis my black cur I am curs-
    ing for not attending on me.   30
Dog. I am that cur.
Elizabeth Sawyer. Thou liest. Hence! Come not nigh me.
Dog. Bow, wow!
Elizabeth Sawyer. Why dost thou thus appear to me in white,
    as if thou wert the ghost of my dear love?   35
Dog. I am dogged, list not to tell thee. Yet, to torment thee,
    my whiteness puts thee in mind of thy winding sheet.
Elizabeth Sawyer. Am I near death?
Dog. Yes, if the dog of hell be near thee. When the devil
    comes to thee as a lamb, have at thy throat!   40
Elizabeth Sawyer. Off, cur!
Dog. He has the back of a sheep but the belly of an otter;
    devours by sea and land. Why am I in white? Didst thou
    not pray to me?
Elizabeth Sawyer. Yes, thou dissembling hell-hound!   45
    Why now in white more than at other times?
Dog. Be blasted with the news! Whiteness is day's foot-boy, a
    forerunner to light which shows thy old rivelled face.

---

21. *powder-mine*] trail of gunpowder.
    34. *Why . . . white*] See Goodcole (p. 143): '**Question.** *In what shape
would the Devil come unto you?* **Answer.** Always in the shape of a dog of two
colours, sometimes of black and sometimes of white.' Cf. the proverb, 'The
white devil is worse than the black'.
    36. *dogged*] cruel, sullenly obstinate. (With a pun on *dog*.)
    list] choose.
    40. *have at*] protect, watch out for.
    47. *blasted*] destroyed.
    foot-boy] page, servant.
    48. *rivelled*] wrinkled.

Villains are stripped naked; the witch must be beaten out
of her cockpit.   50
Elizabeth Sawyer. Must she? She shall not! Thou art a lying
spirit.
Why to mine eyes art thou a flag of truce?
I am at peace with none; 'tis the black colour,
Or none, which I fight under. I do not like
Thy puritan paleness; glowing furnaces   55
Are far more hot than they which flame outright.
If thou my old dog art, go and bite such
As I shall set thee on.
Dog. I will not.
Elizabeth Sawyer. I'll sell my self to twenty thousand fiends   60
To have thee torn in pieces, then.
Dog. Thou canst not. Thou art so ripe to fall into hell that no
more of my kennel will so much as bark at him that hangs
thee.
Elizabeth Sawyer. I shall run mad.   65
Dog. Do so. Thy time is come to curse, and rave, and die.
The glass of thy sins is full, and it must run out at gallows.
Elizabeth Sawyer. It cannot, ugly cur. I'll confess nothing,
And not confessing, who dare come and swear
I have bewitched them? I'll not confess one mouthful.   70
Dog. Choose, and be hanged or burned.
Elizabeth Sawyer. Spite of the devil and thee, I'll muzzle up
my tongue from telling tales.
Dog. Spite of thee and the devil, thou'lt be condemned.
Elizabeth Sawyer. Yes? When?   75
Dog. And ere the executioner catch thee full in's claws,
thou'lt confess all.

---

50. *cockpit*] den; literally, an enclosed arena for cock-fighting, here with a
play on the Cockpit Theatre where the play was performed.

55. *puritan*] i.e. hypocritical.

55-6. *glowing . . . outright*] Proverbial, 'Fire that's closest kept burns most
of all'.

67. *glass*] i.e. a time-keeping glass such as an hour-glass.

71.] i.e. 'Whether you choose to confess or not you will be executed'. See
4.1.72n.

76. *full in's*] fully in his.

Elizabeth Sawyer. Out, dog!

Dog.   Out, witch! Thy trial is at hand.
  Our prey being had, the devil does laughing stand.

> *The* DOG *stands aloof. Enter* OLD BANKS, RATCLIFFE
> *and* Countrymen.

Old Banks. She's here; attach her.—Witch, you must go with   80
  us.

Elizabeth Sawyer. Whither? To hell?

Old Banks. No, no, no, old crone. Your mittimus shall be
  made thither, but your own gaolers shall receive you.—
  Away with her!   [*They seize her.*]   85

Elizabeth Sawyer. My Tommy! My sweet Tom-boy! Oh,
    thou dog!
  Dost thou now fly to thy kennel and forsake me?
  Plagues and consumptions—

                              Exeunt [*all but* DOG].

Dog.   Ha, ha, ha, ha!
  Let not the world witches or devils condemn;
  They follow us, and then we follow them.   90

> [*Enter*] YOUNG BANKS *to the* DOG.

Young Banks. I would fain meet with mine ingle once more.
  He has had a claw amongst 'em. My rival, that loved my
  wench, is like to be hanged like an innocent. A kind cur
  where he takes, but where he takes not, a dogged rascal.
  I know the villain loves me.   [*Dog*] *barks.*   95
  No! Art thou there? That's Tom's voice, but 'tis not he.
  This is a dog of another hair, this. Bark and not speak to

79.] i.e. The devil laughs when his victim is caught.

80. *attach*] arrest.

83. *mittimus*] warrant committing a person to prison.

84. *thither*] i.e. to hell.

90.] i.e. 'Witches offer worship to us devils, and then we pursue them (to damnation)'.

91. *fain*] gladly.

92. *He . . . 'em*] i.e. Tom has been striking out at my rivals.

93. *innocent*] idiot, simpleton, with the secondary sense of an innocent person.

94. *takes*] shows favour.

me? Not Tom, then. There's as much difference betwixt
Tom and this as betwixt white and black.

Dog. Hast thou forgot me?   [*Dog barks.*]   100

Young Banks. That's Tom again. Prithee, ningle, speak. Is thy
name Tom?

Dog. Whilst I served my old Dame Sawyer, 'twas. I'm gone
from her now.

Young Banks. Gone? Away with the witch then, too! She'll   105
never thrive if thou leavest her. She knows no more how
to kill a cow, or a horse, or a sow without thee, than she
does to kill a goose.

Dog. No, she has done killing now, but must be killed for
what she has done. She's shortly to be hanged.   110

Young Banks. Is she? In my conscience, if she be, 'tis thou
hast brought her to the gallows, Tom.

Dog. Right; I served her to that purpose. 'Twas part of my
wages.

Young Banks. This was no honest servant's part, by your   115
leave, Tom. This remember, I pray you: between you and
I, I entertained you ever as a dog, not as a devil.

Dog. True, and so I used thee doggedly, not devilishly. I have
deluded thee for sport to laugh at. The wench thou seekst
after thou never spakst with, but a spirit in her form, habit   120
and likeness. Ha, ha!

Young Banks. I do not then wonder at the change of your
garments, if you can enter into shapes of women too.

Dog. Any shape to blind such silly eyes as thine, but chiefly
those coarse creatures, dog or cat, hare, ferret, frog, toad.   125

Young Banks. Louse or flea?

Dog. Any poor vermin.

Young Banks. It seems you devils have poor thin souls, that

105–8.] This speech is given erroneously to Dog in the quarto text.

106–8. *She . . . goose*] Young Banks's comment reflects the rational scepticism found in Gifford's *A Dialogue*, in which Daniell rigorously argues that
witches are servants of the devil and thus have no power or influence of their
own: 'I know that witches and conjurers are seduced and become the vassals
of Satan: they be his servants, and not he theirs' (sig. B3r).

108. *goose*] also having the sense of 'female simpleton' and sometimes
'prostitute'.

118. *doggedly*] as if I were a dog, i.e. affectionately.

124–6.] See 2.1.36n.

you can bestow yourselves in such small bodies. But pray
you, Tom, one question at parting—I think I shall never   130
see you more—where do you borrow those bodies that
are none of your own? The garment-shape you may hire
at broker's.
Dog. Why wouldst thou know that, fool? It avails thee not.
Young Banks. Only for my mind's sake, Tom, and to tell   135
some of my friends.
Dog. I'll thus much tell thee. Thou never art so distant
  From an evil spirit but that thy oaths,
  Curses, and blasphemies pull him to thine elbow.
  Thou never tellst a lie but that a devil   140
  Is within hearing it; thy evil purposes
  Are ever haunted. But when they come to act—
  As thy tongue slandering, bearing false witness,
  Thy hand stabbing, stealing, cosening, cheating—
  He's then within thee. Thou playst, he bets upon thy
    part.   145
  Although thou lose, yet he will gain by thee.
Young Banks. Ay? Then he comes in the shape of a rook?
Dog. The old cadaver of some self-strangled wretch
  We sometimes borrow, and appear human.
  The carcass of some disease-slain strumpet   150
  We varnish fresh, and wear as her first beauty.
  Didst never hear? If not, it has been done;
  An hot luxurious lecher in his twines,
  When he has thought to clip his dalliance,
  There has provided been for his embrace   155
  A fine hot flaming devil in her place.

---

133. *broker's*] dealer's shop in second-hand furniture and clothes; a pawn-
broker's.

134. *avails thee not*] is of no use to you.

137–46.] See 2.1.128n and Goodcole (Appendix, p. 141), 'The first time
that the Devil came unto me was when I was cursing, swearing and
blaspheming . . . the first words that he spake unto me were these, "Oh! Have
I now found you cursing, swearing and blaspheming? Now you are mine"'.

147. *rook*] cant term for a cheat, swindler or sharper in gaming.

153–6.] Plays dramatising such devilish substitutions include Marston's
Sophonisba and Marlowe's *Dr Faustus*.

153. *twines*] embraces.

154. *clip his dalliance*] embrace his love.

Young Banks. Yes, I am partly a witness to this, but I never
    could embrace her. I thank thee for that, Tom. Well,
    again I thank thee, Tom, for all this counsel; without a
    fee too. There's few lawyers of thy mind now. Certainly,   160
    Tom, I begin to pity thee.
Dog. Pity me! For what?
Young Banks. Were it not possible for thee to become an
    honest dog yet? 'Tis a base life that you lead, Tom, to
    serve witches, to kill innocent children, to kill harmless   165
    cattle, to 'stroy corn and fruit, etc. 'Twere better yet to
    be a butcher and kill for yourself.
Dog. Why? These are all my delights, my pleasures, fool.
Young Banks. Or, Tom, if you could give your mind to duck-
    ing, I know you can swim, fetch and carry, some shop-   170
    keeper in London would take great delight in you and be
    a tender master over you. Or if you have a mind to the
    game either at bull or bear, I think I could prefer you to
    Moll Cutpurse.
Dog. Ha, ha! I should kill all the game, bulls, bears, dogs, and   175
    all, not a cub to be left.
Young Banks. You could do, Tom, but you must play fair;
    you should be staved off else. Or, if your stomach did
    better like to serve in some nobleman's, knight's, or
    gentleman's kitchen, if you could brook the wheel and   180
    turn the spit—your labour could not be much—when
    they have roast meat, that's but once or twice in the week
    at most; here you might lick your own toes very well. Or

---

166. *'stroy*] destroy.

etc.] probably an invitation for the actor to improvise additional topical
malificia.

169–71. *if you . . . in you*] The use of water-spaniels for duck hunting was
a popular pastime for London citizens.

173. *bull or bear*] i.e. bull or bear baiting.

prefer] recommend.

174. *Moll Cutpurse*] Mary Frith (*c.* 1589–1662) adopted male clothes and a
masculine way of life. Noted for her skill with the sword, she was, in later life,
reputed to be a whore, bawd, cutpurse and receiver. She was the heroine of
Middleton and Dekker's *The Roaring Girl* (1610).

178. *staved off*] driven off or beaten with a staff or stave.

180. *brook*] endure.

wheel] treadwheel connected to a roasting spit.

if you could translate yourself into a lady's arming puppy,
there you might lick sweet lips and do many pretty of-   185
fices; but to creep under an old witch's coats and suck
like a great puppy! Fie upon't! I have heard beastly things
of you, Tom.

Dog. Ha, ha! The worse thou heardst of me, the better 'tis.
Shall I serve thee, fool, at the self-same rate?   190

Young Banks. No, I'll see thee hanged; thou shalt be damned
first! I know thy qualities too well. I'll give no suck to
such whelps, therefore henceforth I defy thee. Out and
avaunt!

Dog. Nor will I serve for such a silly soul.   195
I am for greatness now, corrupted greatness.
There I'll shug in, and get a noble countenance;
Serve some Briarean footcloth-strider
That has an hundred hands to catch at bribes,
But not a finger's nail of charity.   200
Such, like the dragon's tail, shall pull down hundreds
To drop and sink with him. I'll stretch myself
And draw this bulk small as a silver wire,
Enter at the least pore tobacco fume
Can make a breach for. Hence, silly fool!   205
I scorn to prey on such an atom soul.

Young Banks. Come out, come out, you cur! I will beat thee

---

184. *arming puppy*] a pet dog carried in a lady's arms as a fashion
accessory.

185–6. *offices*] services (with erotic suggestion).

193–4. *Out and avaunt!*] Away with you, begone!

197. *shug in*] possibly a variant of 'shog' and thus perhaps meaning 'force
one's way in', 'shove in'.

countenance] patronage, position; appearance, demeanour.

198. *Briarean footcloth-strider*] i.e. a corrupt or grasping high placed offi-
cial. Briareus was a hundred-handed giant of Greek mythology; a 'footcloth-
strider' is one who rides a horse covered with a richly worked horsecloth.

201. *dragon's tail*] a Biblical allusion to Revelation, 12.3–4. '. . . and be-
hold a great red dragon having seven heads and ten horns, and seven crowns
upon his heads. And his tail drew the third part of the stars of heaven, and
did cast them to the earth.'

204–5. *Enter . . . for*] an exaggerated notion of thinness. The assumption
appears to be that tobacco smoke can be ingested through the pores of the
skin.

206. *atom*] insignificant, worthless.

out of the bounds of Edmonton, and tomorrow we go in
procession, and after thou shalt never come in again. If
thou goest to London I'll make thee go about by Tyburn,   210
stealing in by Thieving Lane. If thou canst rub thy shoulder against a lawyer's gown as thou passest by
Westminster Hall, do; if not, to the stairs amongst the
bandogs, take water, and the devil go with thee.

Exeunt YOUNG BANKS, DOG *barking.*

5.2

Enter JUSTICE, SIR ARTHUR [CLARINGTON], WARBECK,
[SOMERTON, OLD] CARTER [*and*] KATHERINE.

Justice. Sir Arthur, though the bench hath mildly censured
your errors, yet you have indeed been the instrument that
wrought all their misfortunes. I would wish you paid
down your fine speedily and willingly.

208–9. *we . . . procession*] Young Banks refers to the ceremony of beating
the parish bounds.

210. *Tyburn*] the site of the gallows close to the junction of Oxford Street
and the Edgware Road, London.

211. *Thieving Lane*] a short street in Westminster. It was the way by which
thieves were taken to the Gatehouse prison.

213. *Westminster Hall*] the great hall of Westminster Palace, which housed
the courts of justice and was often used for state trials.

stairs] landing-stage.

214. *bandogs*] ferocious chained-up dogs.

take water] go by water, embark.

1–3. *though . . . misfortunes*] The dramatists leave the audience unclear as
to the precise nature of Sir Arthur's 'errors', though we may surmise that his
prior knowledge of Frank and Winnifride's marriage and thus Frank's subsequent bigamy has been discovered. It also seems clear from the Justice's
remarks (5.3.157–60) that his affair with Winnifride has come to light.
Similarly Old Carter points the finger at Sir Arthur at 5.3.118 and 163–5 as
bearing major responsibility for the tragedy. The dramatists do not explore
Sir Arthur's exposure in court, since their main focus lies elsewhere on the
execution of Elizabeth Sawyer and Frank Thorney. However, the communal
emphasis of the closure requires a recognition of social responsibility at all
levels.

1. *bench*] court; judge.

3. *their*] ambiguous. The reference could be to Frank, Winnifride and
Susan, but may also refer to the accused, Warbeck and Somerton.

Sir Arthur. I'll need no urging to it.   5

Old Carter. If you should, 'twere a shame to you; for, if I
 should speak my conscience, you are worthier to be
 hanged of the two, all things considered; and now make
 what you can of it. But I am glad these gentlemen are
 freed.   10

Warbeck. We knew our innocence.

Somerton.   And therefore feared it not.

Katherine. But I am glad that I have you safe. *Noise within.*

Justice. How now! What noise is that?

Old Carter. Young Frank is going the wrong way. Alas, poor
 youth! Now I begin to pity him.   [*Exeunt.*]   15

5.3

 Enter YOUNG [FRANK] THORNEY *and* [Officers *with*] *halberds*
           [*and exeunt*].

 Enter as to see the execution OLD CARTER, OLD THORNEY,
   KATHERINE, [*and*] WINNIFRIDE *weeping.*

Old Thorney. Here let our sorrows wait him. To press nearer
 The place of his sad death, some apprehensions
 May tempt our grief too much, at height already.
 Daughter, be comforted.

Winnifride.   Comfort and I
 Are too far separated to be joined   5
 But in eternity. I share too much
 Of him that's going thither.

Old Carter.   Poor woman,
 'Twas not thy fault. I grieve to see thee weep

---

14. *going . . . way*] going to the gallows; an allusion to the proverb, 'To go
the wrong way to work'.

0.1–4.] The quarto's stage directions are confusing, since they suggest that
Frank is on stage whilst Old Thorney (l. 1) speaks of his son as though he
were *not* present, and also have Frank enter *again* at l. 53.2 '*to execution*'. It
would seem sensible that Frank and his guards should cross the stage as an
emblematic prologue to the play's closure, to be followed by the entrance of
the other characters.

0.1. halberds] military weapons; sharp-edged blades ending in spear-like
points set upon shafts five to seven feet long.

For him that hath my pity too.

Winnifride. My fault was lust, my punishment was shame.   10
　　Yet I am happy that my soul is free
　　Both from consent, foreknowledge and intent
　　Of any murder but of mine own honour,
　　Restored again by a fair satisfaction,
　　And since not to be wounded.

Old Thorney.　　　　　　　　　Daughter, grieve not   15
　　For what necessity forceth; rather resolve
　　To conquer it with patience.—
　　Alas, she faints!

Winnifride.　　　　My griefs are strong upon me.
　　My weakness scarce can bear them.

[*Voices.*] (*Within*) Away with her! Hang her! Witch!   20

　　　　Enter [ELIZABETH] SAWYER *to execution*, Officers *with*
　　　　　　　halberds, [*and*] Country-people.

Old Carter. The witch, that instrument of mischief! Did not
　　she witch the devil into my son-in-law when he killed my
　　poor daughter?—Do you hear, Mother Sawyer?

Elizabeth Sawyer. What would you have? Cannot a poor old
　　woman
　　Have your leave to die without vexation?   25

Old Carter. Did you not bewitch Frank to kill his wife? He
　　could never have done't without the devil.

Elizabeth Sawyer. Who doubts it? But is every devil mine?
　　Would I had one now whom I might command
　　To tear you all in pieces! Tom would have done't   30
　　Before he left me.

Old Carter. Thou didst bewitch Anne Ratcliffe to kill herself.

Elizabeth Sawyer. Churl, thou liest! I never did her hurt.
　　Would you were all as near your ends as I am,
　　That gave evidence against me for it.   35

---

14. *satisfaction*] penance, atonement.

15. *since*] since then.

15–16. *grieve . . . forceth*] Cf. the proverb 'Never grieve for what you cannot help'.

28.] Elizabeth Sawyer can have no knowledge of the Dog's involvement in
Susan's murder, although she has allowed the devil to penetrate the community of Edmonton.

First Countryman. I'll be sworn, Master Carter, she bewitched
     Gammer Washbowl's sow to cast her pigs a day before
     she would have farrowed, yet they were sent up to
     London, and sold for as good Westminster dog-pigs at
     Bartholomew Fair as ever great-bellied ale-wife longed   40
     for.
Elizabeth Sawyer. These dogs will mad me. I was well
          resolved
     To die in my repentance. Though 'tis true
     I would live longer if I might, yet since
     I cannot, pray torment me not; my conscience   45
     Is settled as it shall be. All take heed
     How they believe the devil; at last he'll cheat you.
Old Carter. Thou'dst best confess all truly.
Elizabeth Sawyer.   Yet again?
     Have I scarce breath enough to say my prayers,
     And would you force me to spend that in bawling?   50
     Bear witness. I repent all former evil;
     There is no damnèd conjuror like the devil.
All. Away with her! Away!
                    [*Exeunt* ELIZABETH SAWYER *with* Officers.]

     Enter FRANK [THORNEY] *to execution,* Officers, JUSTICE,
     SIR ARTHUR [CLARINGTON], WARBECK [*and*] SOMERTON.

---

37. *cast*] give birth to.

38. *farrowed*] delivered her piglets.

39. *Westminster dog-pigs*] male or boar pigs. Pigs sold at Bartholomew
Fair, held in Smithfield on 24 August, were called Bartholomew-boar-pigs,
but the reference to Westminster pigs is obscure.

40–1. *Bartholomew . . . for*] The craving of pregnant women for
Bartholomew Fair roast pig is dramatised in Jonson's *Bartholomew Fair*
(1614), 1.5.48–56 and 1.6.19–41 (Revels ed.).

42. *dogs*] worthless, despicable or cowardly people. The word also recalls
Sawyer's association with her familiar.

mad me] drive me mad.

43. *in my repentance*] i.e. in a state of repentance.

43–6. *Though . . . be*] Cf. Goodcole (see Appendix, p. 147) '**Question**.
*What moves you now to make this confession? Did any urge you to it or bid you do
it? Is it for any hope of life you do it?* **Answer**. No, I do it to clear my
conscience. And now having done it I am the more quiet and the better
prepared, and willing thereby to suffer death. For I have no hope at all of my
life although, I must confess, I would live longer if I might.'

Old Thorney. Here's the sad object which I yet must meet
    With hope of comfort, if a repentant end   55
    Make him more happy than misfortune would
    Suffer him here to be.
Frank Thorney.   Good sirs, turn from me.
    You will revive affliction almost killed
    With my continual sorrow.
Old Thorney.   O Frank, Frank!
    Would I had sunk in mine own wants, or died   60
    But one bare minute ere thy fault was acted!
Frank Thorney. To look upon your sorrows executes me
    Before my execution.
Winnifride.   Let me pray you, sir—
Frank Thorney. Thou much wronged woman, I must sigh
    for thee
    As he that's only loath to leave the world   65
    For that he leaves thee in it unprovided,
    Unfriended; and for me to beg a pity
    From any man to thee when I am gone
    Is more than I can hope; nor, to say truth,
    Have I deserved it. But there is payment   70
    Belongs to goodness from the great exchequer
    Above; it will not fail thee, Winnifride.
    Be that thy comfort.
Old Thorney.   Let it be thine too,
    Untimely-lost young man.
Frank Thorney.   He is not lost
    Who bears his peace within him. Had I spun   75
    My web of life out at full length, and dreamed
    Away my many years in lusts, in surfeits,
    Murders of reputations, gallant sins
    Commended or approved; then, though I had
    Died easily, as great and rich men do,   80
    Upon my own bed, not compelled by justice,
    You might have mourned for me indeed; my miseries
    Had been as everlasting as remediless.

---

57. *Suffer him here*] allow him on this earth.
66. *For that*] because.
70. *payment*] reward.
71–2. *great exchequer / Above*] i.e. God.

But now the law hath not arraigned, condemned
With greater rigour my unhappy fact   85
Than I myself have every little sin
My memory can reckon from my childhood.
A court hath been kept here where I am found
Guilty; the difference is, my impartial judge
Is much more gracious than my faults   90
Are monstrous to be named, yet they are monstrous.
Old Thorney. Here's comfort in this penitence.
Winnifride.   It speaks
How truly you are reconciled, and quickens
My dying comfort that was near expiring
With my last breath. Now this repentance makes thee   95
As white as innocence, and my first sin with thee,
Since which I knew none like it, by my sorrow
Is clearly cancelled. Might our souls together
Climb to the height of their eternity,
And there enjoy what earth denied us, happiness!   100
But since I must survive and be the monument
Of thy loved memory, I will preserve it
With a religious care, and pay thy ashes
A widow's duty, calling that end best
Which, though it stain the name, makes the soul blest.   105
Frank Thorney. Give me thy hand, poor woman.
     [*He takes her hand.*]   Do not weep.
Farewell. Thou dost forgive me?
Winnifride.   'Tis my part
To use that language.
Frank Thorney.   Oh, that my example
Might teach the world hereafter what a curse
Hangs on their heads who rather choose to marry   110
A goodly portion than a dower of virtues!
Are you there, gentlemen? There is not one
Amongst you whom I have not wronged; [*To Old Carter*]
     you most.
I robbed you of a daughter, but she is

---

85. *fact*] crime.
93. *quickens*] gives life to.
101. *monument*] living reminder.
111. *goodly portion*] rich dowry.

In heaven, and I must suffer for it willingly.   115
Old Carter. Ay, ay, she's in heaven, and I am glad to see thee
    so well prepared to follow her. I forgive thee with all my
    heart. If thou hadst not had ill counsel thou wouldst not
    have done as thou didst; the more shame for them.
Somerton. [*To Frank*] Spare your excuse to me; I do conceive   120
    What you would speak. I would you could as easily
    Make satisfaction to the law as to my wrongs.
    I am sorry for you.
Warbeck.   And so am I,
    And heartily forgive you.
Katherine.   I will pray for you
    For her sake, who I am sure did love you dearly.   125
Sir Arthur. Let us part friendly too. I am ashamed
    Of my part in thy wrongs.
Frank Thorney.   You are all merciful,
    And send me to my grave in peace.—Sir Arthur,
    Heavens send you a new heart!—Lastly to you, sir;
    And though I have deserved not to be called   130
    Your son, yet give me leave upon my knees
    To beg a blessing.   [*He kneels.*]
Old Thorney.   Take it. Let me wet
    Thy cheeks with the last tears my griefs have left me.
    Oh, Frank, Frank, Frank!
Frank Thorney.   Let me beseech you, gentlemen,
    To comfort my old father. Keep him with ye;   135
    Love this distressèd widow, and as often
    As you remember what a graceless man
    I was, remember likewise that these are
    Both free, both worthy of a better fate
    Than such a son or husband as I have been.   140
    All help me with your prayers. On, on, 'tis just
    That law should purge the guilt of blood and lust.
                            Exit [*with* Officers].
Old Carter. Go thy ways. I did not think to have shed one tear
    for thee, but thou hast made me water my plants spite of
    my heart.—Master Thorney, cheer up, man. Whilst I can   145
    stand by you, you shall not want help to keep you from

---

139. *free*] i.e. innocent.

falling. We have lost our children, both on's the wrong
way, but we cannot help it. Better or worse, 'tis now as
'tis.

Old Thorney. I thank you, sir. You are more kind than I   150
Have cause to hope or look for.

Old Carter. Master Somerton, is Kate yours or no?

Somerton. We are agreed.

Katherine.   And but my faith is passed,
I should fear to be married. Husbands are
So cruelly unkind. Excuse me that   155
I am thus troubled.

Somerton.   Thou shalt have no cause.

Justice. Take comfort, Mistress Winnifride. Sir Arthur,
For his abuse to you and to your husband,
Is by the bench enjoined to pay you down
A thousand marks.

Sir Arthur.   Which I will soon discharge.   160

Winnifride. Sir, 'tis too great a sum to be employed
Upon my funeral.

Old Carter. Come, come. If luck had served, Sir Arthur, and
every man had his due, somebody might have tottered ere
this without paying fines, like it as you list.—Come to me,   165
Winnifride; shalt be welcome.—Make much of her, Kate,
I charge you. I do not think but she's a good wench and
hath had wrong as well as we. So, let's every man home
to Edmonton with heavy hearts, yet as merry as we can,
though not as we would.   170

Justice. Join, friends, in sorrow, make of all the best.
Harms past may be lamented, not redressed.   *Exeunt.*

---

147. *on's*] of us.

153. *but . . . passed*] if my love were not pledged.

157–60. *Take . . . marks*] The quarto's assigning of these lines to Old
Carter seems inappropriate, since he habitually speaks in prose and the
subject matter is more suited to the Justice.

160. *thousand marks*] a considerable sum; a mark was worth thirteen
shillings and fourpence, i.e. two-thirds of a pound sterling.

164. *tottered*] swung to and fro, especially at the end of a rope. The
reference is to Sir Arthur, as the comment on 'fines' emphasises.

165. *like . . . list*] take it or leave it.

167. *charge*] order, command.

EPILOGUE

Winnifride. I am a widow still, and must not sort
    A second choice without a good report,
    Which though some widows find, and few deserve,
    Yet I dare not presume, but will not swerve
    From modest hopes. All noble tongues are free;   5
    The gentle may speak one kind word for me.

                               PHEN.

FINIS.

---

1. *sort*] choose, select.

2. *report*] reputation.

6. *gentle*] well-bred, cultivated. A conventional compliment to the audience.

7. PHEN] i.e. Ezekiel Fenn, a boy actor with Queen Henrietta's Company who took the part of Winnifride and subsequently became a leading member of Beeston's Company at the Cockpit.

Appendix: source material

The wonderful discovery of Elizabeth Sawyer, a Witch, late of Edmonton, her conviction and condemnation and death.

Together with the relation of the Devil's access to her and their conference together.

Written by Henry Goodcole, Minister of the Word of God, and her continual visitor in the Gaol of Newgate.

Published by Authority.

London, Printed for William Butler, and are to be sold at his shop in Saint Dunstan's Churchyard Fleet Street. 1621.

Goodcole's pamphlet is presented with modernised spelling, but the punctuation of the original has been retained.

The Author's Apology to the Christian readers, who wisheth
to them all health and happiness.

The publication of this subject whereof I now write hath been by
importunity extorted from me, who would have been content to
have concealed it knowing the diversity of opinions concerning
things of this nature and that not among the ignorant, but among
some of the learned. For my part I meddle herewith nothing but
matter of fact, and to that end pro[cure?] the testimony of the living
and the dead, which I hope shall be authentical for the confirmation
of this narration and free me from all censorious minds and mouths.
It is none of my intent here to discuss or dispute of witches or
witchcraft, but desire most therein to be dispensed with all, knowing
that, in such a little treatise as this is, no matter that can be effectual
therein can be comprised, especially in so short a time of deliberation as three or four days. And the rather do I now publish this to
purchase my peace which without it being done I could scarce at any
time be at quiet, for many who would take no nay but still desired of
me written copies of this ensuing declaration. Another reason was to
defend the truth of the cause which, in some measure, hath received
a wound already by most base and false ballads which were sung at
the time of our returning from the witch's execution. In them I was
ashamed to see and hear such ridiculous fictions of her bewitching
corn on the ground, of a ferret and an owl daily sporting before her,
of the bewitched woman braining herself, of the spirits attending in
the prison; all which I knew to be fitter for an ale-bench than for a
relation of proceeding in Court of Justice. And thereupon I wonder
that such lewd ballad-mongers should be suffered to creep into the
printers' presses and people's ears.

And so I rest at your opinions and judgements

Your well-wisher in the Lord Jesus,

Henry Goodcole

A true declaration of the manner of proceeding against
Elizabeth Sawyer, late of Edmonton, Spinster,
and the evidence of her conviction.

A great and long suspicion was held of this person to be a witch and the eye of Mr. Arthur Robinson, a worthy Justice of the Peace who dwelleth at Totnam near to her, was watchful over her and her ways, and that not without just cause, still having his former long suspicion of her by the information of her neighbours that dwelt about her; from suspicion to proceed to great presumptions, seeing the death of nurse-children and cattle strangely and suddenly to happen. And to find out who should be the author of this mischief an old ridiculous custom was used which was to pluck the thatch of her house and to burn it, and it being so burned the author of such mischief should presently then come; and it was observed and affirmed to the Court that Elizabeth Sawyer would presently frequent the house of them that burnt the thatch which they plucked of her house, and come without any sending for.

This trial, though it was slight and ridiculous, yet it settled a resolution in those whom it concerned to find out by all means they could endeavour her long and close-carried witchery, to explain it to the world and, being descried, to pay in the end such a worker of iniquity her wages and that which she had deserved, namely shame and death, from which the Devil, that had so long deluded her, did not come as she said to show the least help of his unto her to deliver her. But being descried in his ways and works, immediately he fled leaving her to shift and answer for herself, with public and private marks on her body as followeth:

1. Her face was most pale and ghost-like without any blood at all, and her countenance was still dejected to the ground.

2. Her body was crooked and deformed, even bending together, which so happened but a little before her apprehension.

3. That tongue which by cursing, swearing, blaspheming and imprecating, as afterward she confessed, was the occasioning cause of the Devil's access unto her, even at that time, and to claim her thereby as his own by it discovered her lying, swearing and blaspheming. As also evident proofs produced against her, to stop her mouth with Truth's authority, at which hearing she was not able to speak a sensible or ready word for her defence, but sends out in the hearing of the Judge, jury and all good people that stood by many most fearful imprecations for destruction against herself then to

happen, as heretofore she had wished and endeavoured to happen on divers of her neighbours. The which the righteous Judge of Heaven, whom she thus invocated to judge then and discern her cause, did reveal.

Thus God did wonderfully overtake her in her own wickedness to make her tongue to be the means of her own destruction which had destroyed many before.

And in this manner, namely that out of her false swearing, the truth whereof she little thought should be found but by her swearing and cursing blended, it thus far made against her that both Judge and jury, all of them, grew more and more suspicious of her and not without great cause. For none that had the fear of God or any the least motion of God's grace left in them would or durst to presume so impudently with execrations and false oaths to affront justice.

On Saturday, being the fourteenth day of April *Anno Dom.* 1621 this Elizabeth Sawyer, late of Edmonton in the County of Middlesex spinster, was arraigned and indited three several times at Justice Hall in the Old Bailey in London in the parish of Saint Sepulcher's in the Ward of Farrington Without, which indictments were *viz*:

That she the said Elizabeth Sawyer, not having the fear of God before her eyes but moved and seduced by the Devil, by diabolical help did out of her malicious heart, because her neighbours where she dwelt would not buy brooms of her, would therefore thus revenge herself on them in this manner, namely, witch to death their nurse children and cattle. But for brevity's sake I here omit forms of law and informations.

She was also indicted for that she, the said Elizabeth Sawyer, by diabolical help and out of her malice aforethought, did witch unto death Agnes Ratcleife, a neighbour of hers dwelling in the town of Edmonton where she did likewise dwell, and the cause that urged her thereunto was because that Agnes Ratcleife did strike a sow of hers in her sight for licking up a little soap where she had laid it, and for that Elizabeth Sawyer would be revenged of her and thus threatened Agnes Ratcleife that it should be a dear blow unto her, which accordingly fell out and suddenly. For that evening Agnes Ratcleife fell very sick and was extraordinarily vexed and in a most strange manner in her sickness was tormented. Oath whereof was by this Agnes Ratcleife's husband given to the Court; the time when she fell sick and the time when she died, which was within four days after she fell sick. And further then related that in the time of her sickness his wife, Agnes Ratcleife, lay foaming at the mouth and was extraordinarily distempered which, many of his neighbours seeing as well as himself, bred suspicion in them that some mischief was done against her, and by none else but alone by this Elizabeth Sawyer it was done. Concerning whom the said Agnes Ratcleife, lying on her death-bed, these words confidently spake, namely, that if she did die at that time she would verily take it on her death that Elizabeth Sawyer, her neighbour, whose sow with a washing-beetle she had stricken, and so for that cause her malice being great was the occasion of her death.

To prove her innocency she put herself to the trial of God and the Country, and what care was taken both by the honourable Bench and jury the judicious standers-by can witness; and God knows who will reward it.

The jury hearing this evidence, given upon oath by the husband of the above-named Agnes Ratcleife and his wife's speeches relating to them likewise an [on] oath as she lay on her death-bed, to be truth that she had said unto her husband, namely that if she died at that time she, the said Elizabeth Sawyer, was the cause of her death and maliciously did by her witchery procure the same.

This made some impression in their minds and caused due and mature deliberation, not trusting their own judgements what to do in a matter of such great import as life they deemed might be conserved.

The foreman of the jury asked of Master Heneage Finch, Recorder, his direction and advice, to whom he, Christianlike thus replied, namely, 'Do in it as God shall put in your hearts'.

Master Arthur Robinson, a worshipful Justice of Peace dwelling at Totnam, had often and divers times, upon the complaints of the neighbours against this Elizabeth Sawyer, laboriously and carefully examined her and still his suspicion was strengthened against her that doubtless she was a witch. An information was given unto him by some of her neighbours that this Elizabeth Sawyer had a private and strange mark on her body by which their suspicion was confirmed against her, and he, sitting in the Court at that time of her trial, informed the Bench thereof, desiring the Bench to send for women to search her presently before the jury, did go forth to bring in the verdict concerning Elizabeth Sawyer whether that she was guilty or no. To which motion of his they most willingly condescended.

The Bench commanded officers appointed for those purposes to fetch in three women to search the body of Elizabeth Sawyer to see if they could find any such unwonted mark as they were informed of. One of the women's names was Margaret Weaver that keeps the Sessions' House for the City of London, a widow of an honest reputation; and two other grave matrons brought in by the Officer out of the street, passing by there by chance, were joined with her in this search of the person named who, fearing and perceiving she should by that search of theirs be then discovered, behaved herself most sluttishly and loathsomely towards them, intending thereby to prevent their search of her, which my pen would forbear to write these things for modesty's sake but I would not vary in what was delivered to the Bench, expressly and openly spoken. Yet, nevertheless, niceness they laid aside and, according to the request of the Court and to that trust reposed in them by the Bench, they all three severally searched her and made severally their answer unto the Court, being sworn thereunto to deliver the truth. And they all three said that they a little above the fundament of Elizabeth Sawyer, the prisoner there indicted before the Bench for a witch, found a thing like a teat, the bigness of the little finger and the length of half a finger which was branched at the top like a teat and seemed as though one had sucked it, and that the bottom thereof was blue and the top of it was red. This view of theirs and answer that she had such a thing about her, which boldly she denied, gave some insight to the jury of her who, upon their consciences, returned the said Elizabeth Sawyer to be guilty, by diabolical help, of the death of Agnes Ratcleife only and acquitted her of the other two indictments. And thus much of the means that brought her to her deserved death and destruction.

I will address to inform you of her preparation to death which is alone pertinent to my function and declare unto you her confession *verbatim* out of her own mouth, delivered to me the Tuesday after her conviction, though with great labour it was extorted from her; and the same confession I read unto her at the place of her execution. And there she confessed to all people that were there the same to be most true which I shall here relate.

And because it should not be thought that from me alone this proceeded I would have other testimony thereof to stop all contradictions of so palpable a verity that heard her deliver it from her own mouth in the Chapel of Newgate the same time.

In testimony whereof the persons that were then present with me at her confession have hereunto put to their hands and, if it be required further to confirm this to be a truth, will be ready at all times to make oath thereof.

A true relation of the confession of Elizabeth Sawyer, spinster, after her conviction of witchery, taken on Tuesday the 17 day of April, Anno 1621 in the Gaol of Newgate where she was prisoner, then in the presence and hearing of divers persons whose names to verify the same are here subscribed to this ensuing confession; made unto me, Henry Goodcole, Minister of the word of God, Ordinary and Visitor for the Gaol of Newgate. In dialogue manner are here expressed the persons that she murdered and the cattle that she destroyed by the help of the Devil.

In this manner was I enforced to speak unto her because she might understand me and give unto me answer according to my demands, for she was a very ignorant woman.

Question.
By what means came you to have acquaintance with the Devil and when was the first time that you saw him, and how did you know it was the Devil?

Answer.
The first time that the Devil came unto me was when I was cursing, swearing and blaspheming; he then rushed in upon me and never before that time did I see him or he me, and when he, namely the Devil, came to me the first words that he spake unto me were these, 'Oh! Have I now found you cursing, swearing and blaspheming? Now you are mine'. &[1] A wonderful warning to many whose tongues are too frequent in these abominable sins. I pray God that this her terrible example may deter them to leave and distaste them, to put their tongues to a more holy language than the accursed language of hell. The tongue of man is the glory of man and it was ordained to glorify God; but worse than brute beasts they are who have a tongue as well as men that therewith they at once both bless and curse.

Question.
What said you to the Devil when he came unto you and spake unto you; were you not afraid of him? If you did fear him, what said the Devil unto you?

---

1. 'A gentleman, by name Mr. Maddox, standing by and hearing of her say the word blaspheming, did ask of her three or four times whether the Devil said "Have I found you blaspheming", and she confidently said, "Ay".' [Marginal note.]

Answer.

I was in a very great fear when I saw the Devil, but he did bid me not to fear him at all for he would do me no hurt at all but would do for me whatsoever I should require of him, and as he promised unto me he always did such mischiefs as I did bid him to do, both on the bodies of Christians and beasts. If I did bid him vex them to death, as oftentimes I did so bid him, it was then presently by him so done.

Question.

Whether would the Devil bring unto you word or no what he had done for you at your command and, if he did bring you word, how long would it be before he would come unto you again to tell you?

Answer.

He would always bring unto me word what he had done for me within the space of a week. He never failed me at that time and would likewise do it to creatures and beasts two manner of ways, which was by scratching or pinching of them.

Question.

Of what Christians and beasts, and how many were the number that you were the cause of their death, and what moved you to persecute them to the death?

Answer.

I have been, by the help of the Devil, the means of many Christians' and beasts' death. The cause that moved me to do it was malice and envy, for if anybody had angered me in any manner I would be so revenged of them and of their cattle. And do now further confess that I was the cause of those two nurse-children's death for the which I was now indicted and acquitted by the jury.

Question.

Whether did you procure the death of Agnes Ratcleife for which you were found guilty by the jury?

Answer.

No, I did not by my means procure against her the least hurt.

Question.

How long is it since the Devil and you had acquaintance together, and how oftentimes in the week would he come and see you and you company with him?

Answer.

It is eight years since our first acquaintance, and three times in the week, the Devil would come and see me. After such his acquaintance gotten of me, he would come sometimes in the morning and sometimes in the evening.

Question.

In what shape would the Devil come unto you?

Answer.

Always in the shape of a dog of two colours, sometimes of black and sometimes of white.

Question.

What talk had the Devil and you together when that he appeared to you, and what did he ask of you and what did you desire of him?

Answer.

He asked of me, when he came unto me, how I did and what he should do for me, and demanded of me my soul and body, threatening then to tear me in pieces if that I did not grant unto him my soul and my body which he asked of me.

Question.

What did you after such the Devil's asking of you to have your soul and body and after this his threatening of you? Did you for fear grant unto the Devil his desires?

Answer.

Yes, I granted for fear unto the Devil his request of my soul and body; and to seal this my promise made unto him I then gave him leave to suck my blood, the which he asked of me.

Question.

In what place of your body did the Devil suck of your blood, and whether did he himself choose the place or did you yourself appoint him the place? Tell the truth I charge you, as your [you] will answer unto the Almighty God, and tell the reason, if that you can, why he would suck your blood.[2]

2. 'I demanded this question of her to confirm the women's search of her concerning that she had such a mark about her which they, upon their oaths, informed the Court that truth it was she had such a mark. This I asked of her very earnestly, and she thus answered me without any studying for an answer.' [Marginal note.]

Answer.

The place where the Devil sucked my blood was a little above my fundament, and that place chosen by himself. And in that place, by continual drawing, there is a thing in the form of a teat at which the Devil would suck me. And I asked the Devil why he would suck my blood and he said it was to nourish him.

Question.

Whether did you pull up your coats or no when the Devil came to suck you?

Answer.

No, I did not. But the Devil would put his head under my coats and I did willingly suffer him to do what he would.

Question.

How long would the time be that the Devil would continue sucking of you, and whether did you endure any pain the time that he was sucking of you?

Answer.

He would be sucking of me the continuance of a quarter of an hour, and when he sucked me I then felt no pain at all.

Question.

What was the meaning that the Devil when he came unto you would sometimes speak and sometimes bark?[3]

Answer.

It is thus; when the Devil spake to me then he was ready to do for me what I would bid him to do, and when he came barking to me he then had done the mischief that I did bid him to do for me.

Question.

By what name did you call the Devil and what promises did he make to you?

Answer.

I did call the Devil by the name of Tom and he promised to do for me whatsoever I should require of him.

---

3. 'I asked this question because she said that the Devil did not always speak to her.' [Marginal note.]

Question.

What were those two ferrets that you were feeding on a form with white bread and milk when divers children came and saw you feeding of them?[4]

Answer.

I never did any such thing.

Question.

What was the white thing that did run through the thatch of your house? Was it a spirit or devil?[5]

Answer.

So far as I know it was nothing else but a white ferret.

Question.

Did anybody else know but yourself alone of the Devil's coming unto you, and of your practices? Speak the truth and tell the reason why you did not reveal it to your husband or to some other friend?

Answer.

I did not tell anybody thereof that the Devil came unto me, neither I durst not, for the Devil charged me that I should not, and said that if I did tell it to anybody at his next coming to me he then would tear me in pieces.

Question.

Did the Devil at any time find you praying when he came unto you, and did not the Devil forbid you to pray to Jesus Christ but to him alone? And did not he bid you pray to him, the Devil, as he taught you?[6]

Answer.[7]

Yes, he found me once praying and asked of me to whom I prayed and I answered him, 'To Jesus Christ', and he charged me then to

4. 'I asked this of her because that some children of a good bigness and reasonable understanding informed the Court that they had divers times seen her feed two white ferrets with white bread and milk.' [Marginal note.]

5. 'I asked this question of her because her husband testified to the Bench he saw such a white thing run through the thatch of the house and that he catched at it but could not get it, and he thought it was a white ferret.' [Marginal note.]

6. 'Upon my general suspicion I asked of her this question.' [Marginal note.]

7. 'I do here relate the selfsame words upon this question propounded unto her, what prayer the Devil taught her to say.' [Marginal note.]

pray no more to Jesus Christ but to him the Devil and he, the Devil, taught me this prayer: *Sanctibicetur nomen tuum.* (i.e. 'sacred be thy name') Amen.

Question.

Were you ever taught these Latin words before by any person else or did you ever hear it before of anybody, or can you say any more of it?

Answer.

No, I was not taught it by anybody else but by the Devil alone; neither do I understand the meaning of these words nor can speak any more Latin words.

Question.

Did the Devil ask of you the next time he came unto you whether that you used to pray unto him in that manner as he taught you?

Answer.

Yes, at his next coming to me he asked of me if that I did pray unto him as he had taught me, and I answered him again that sometimes I did and sometimes I did not. And the Devil then thus threatened me, 'It is not good for me to mock him'.

Question.

How long is it since you saw the Devil last?

Answer.

It is three weeks since I saw the Devil.

Question.

Did the Devil never come unto you since you were in prison? Speak the truth, as you will answer unto Almighty God.[8]

Answer.

The Devil never came unto me since I was in prison nor, I thank God, I have no motion of him in my mind since I came to prison, neither do I now fear him at all.

Question.

How came your eye to be put out?[9]

8. 'I asked this question because it was rumoured that the Devil came to her since her conviction, and shamelessly printed and openly sung in a ballad, to which many give too much credit.' [Marginal note.]

9. 'The reason why I asked this was because her father and mother's eye, one of theirs was out.' [Marginal note.]

Answer.

With a stick which one of my children had in the hand. That night my mother did die it was done, for I was stooping by the bedside and I, by chance, did hit my eye on the sharp end of the stick.

Question.

Did you ever handle the Devil when he came unto you?[10]

Answer.

Yes, I did stroke him on the back and then he would beck unto me as being therewith contented.

Question.

Would the Devil come unto you all in one bigness?

Answer.

No, when he came unto me in the black shape he then was biggest, and in the white the least; and when that I was praying he then would come unto me in the white colour.

Question.

Why did you at your trial forswear all this that you now do confess?

Answer.

I did it thereby hoping to avoid shame.

Question.

Is all this truth which you have spoken here unto me and that I have now written?

Answer.

Yes, it is all truth, as I shall make answer unto Almighty God.

Question.

What moves you now to make this confession? Did any urge you to it or bid you do it? Is it for any hope of life you do it?

Answer.

No, I do it to clear my conscience. And now having done it I am the more quiet and the better prepared, and willing thereby to suffer death. For I have no hope at all of my life although, I must confess, I would live longer if I might.

10. 'I asked of her this question because some might think this was a visible delusion of her sight only.' [Marginal note.]

A relation what she said at the place of execution which was at Tyburn, on Thursday the 19 day of April 1621.

All this being by her thus freely confessed after her conviction in the Gaol of Newgate on Tuesday the 17 day of April, I acquainted Master Recorder of London therewith who thus directed me to take that her confession with me to the place of execution and to read it to her and to ask of her whether that was truth which she had delivered to me in the prison on Tuesday last. Concerning what she said and how she died I will relate unto you.

'Elizabeth Sawyer, you are now come unto the place of execution. Is that all true which you confessed unto me on Tuesday last when that you were in prison? I have it here and will now read it unto you as you spake it then unto me out of your own mouth; and, if it be true, confess it now to God and to all the people that are here present.'

Answer.

This confession which is now read unto me by Master Henry Goodcole, Minister, with my own mouth I spake it to him on Tuesday last at Newgate, and I here do acknowledge to all the people that are here present that it is all truth, desiring you all to pray unto Almighty God to forgive me my grievous sins.

Question.
By what means hope you now to be saved?

Answer.
By Jesus Christ alone.

Question.
Will you now pray unto Almighty God to forgive unto you all your misdeeds?

Answer.
Ay, with all my heart and mind.

This was confirmed in the hearing of many hundreds, at her last breath, what formerly she in prison confessed to me and at that time spake more heartily than the day before of her execution; on whose body Law was justly inflicted, but mercy in God's power reserved to bestow when and where He pleaseth.

My labour thus ended concerning her, to testify and avouch to the world and all opposers hereof this to be true, those that were present with me in the prison that heard her confession I have desired here their testimonies which is as followeth:

We whose names are here subscribed do thereby testify that Elizabeth Sawyer, late of Edmonton in the County of Middlesex, spinster, did in our hearing confess on Tuesday the 17 of April in the Gaol of Newgate to Master Henry Goodcole, Minister of the Word of God, the repeated foul crimes and confirmed it at her death, the 19 of April following to be true. And if we be thereunto required will be ready to make faith of the truth thereof, namely that this was her confession being alive and a little before her death.

Conclusion.

Dear Christians, lay this to heart. Namely the cause and first time that the Devil came unto her; then, even then when she was cursing, swearing and blaspheming. The Devil rageth and malice reigneth in the hearts of many. O let it not do so! For here you may see the fruits thereof; that it is a plain way to bring you to the Devil; nay, that it brings the Devil to you. For it seemed that when she so fearfully did swear her oaths did so conjure him that he must leave then his mansion place and come at this wretch's command and will, which was by her imprecations. Stand on your guard and watch with sobriety to resist him, the Devil your adversary, who waiteth on you continually to subvert you; that so you that do detest her abominable words and ways may never taste of the cup nor wages of shame and destruction, of which she did in this life; from which and from whose power, Lord Jesus save and defend thy little flock. Amen.